Dying with Dignity

Dying with Dignity

A Plea for Personal Responsibility

Hans Küng and Walter Jens

with contributions by Dietrich Niethammer
and Albin Eser

CONTINUUM   NEW YORK

The Continuum Publishing Company
370 Lexington Avenue
New York, NY 10017

Translated by John Bowden from the German
Copyright © *Menschenwürdig Sterben. Ein Plädoyer
für Selbstverantwortung*
© R. Piper GmbH & Co. KG, Munich 1995
Translation © John Bowden 1995

Printed in the United States of America

Library of Congress Cataloging-in-Publication Data
Küng, Hans, 1928–
[Menschenwürdig sterben. English]
Dying with dignity : a plea for personal responsibility / Hans
Küng and Walter Jens with contributions by Dietrich Niethammer and
Albin Eser ; [translated by John Bowden].
p.   cm.
Includes bibliographical references.
ISBN 0-8264-0885-0 (hdb)
1. Euthanasia—Moral and ethical aspects.   2. Euthanasia—
Religious aspects—Christianity.   3. Assisted suicide—Moral and
ethical aspects.   4. Right to die.   5. Death in literature.
I. Jens, Walter, 1923–   . II. Title.
R726.K8613   1996
179'.7—dc20   95-51978
CIP

Contents

The Dignity and Indignity of Dying as Illuminated by Literature
'If You Want Life, Prepare for Death'

Walter Jens

Discussion

Dignified Dying from a Doctor's Perspective

Dietrich Niethammer

The Possibilities and Limits of Help in Dying:
A Lawyer's View

Albin Eser

An Open Discussion

*Hans Küng, Walter Jens, Dietrich Niethammer,
Albin Eser*

Contents

Introduction

May a seventy-two-year-old woman, with irreparable brain damage after a cardiac arrest, who is lying in a coma and needs to be fed on a drip, have the drip stopped after three years so that she can finally go to sleep in peace? Yes, her son thought, and so did the doctor who was treating her. No, said the nursing staff of the hospital; they did not follow the doctor's instructions, but appealed to the law. As a result the drip feeding was continued. And so this woman, who was totally unresponsive, continued in a coma for a further nine months until she could finally die.

Is such a procedure meaningful, morally responsible? Is such a procedure – and this is primarily a question for legal specialists – required by the law? Yes, said the court in whose jurisdiction the case lay, and fined both the doctor and the son 4800 DM and 6400 DM respectively for attempted murder. No, said the federal court in Karlsruhe, which referred the case to another chamber of the state jurisdiction. The reason given was that the court had illegitimately ignored the wish of the patient, who eight years before her death had already expressed a wish for treatment to be stopped in certain circumstances.

For doctors, nursing staff, lawyers and courts, this decision by the federal court means that more attention must be paid to the wishes of the patient than before, even in cases where the patient can no longer communicate at the time. It is understandable that after this judgment patients' associations recommended that patients should make advance directives ('wills') in which they themselves determine whether or not they want measures to be taken to prolong life in the last phase of their dying. Certainly the decision of the federal court applies only to so-called 'passive' help in dying, e.g. switching off a drip feed and thus shortening life. But in the light of this decision, must not so-called 'active' help in dying also be discussed once more, if greater attention is to be paid to the will of the patient?

When we, a theologian and a literary critic, discussed the question of a dignified dying on a series of evenings before an unexpectedly large audience of men and women, both older and younger, the judgment of the federal court had not yet been given. In any case, neither of us wanted to present ourselves as lawyers. However, we can feel that our basic approach, arguing for human responsibility not only for living but also for dying, was confirmed by this judgment.

In this approach we raised questions both for the law and for medicine, and did not look for easy conversation partners.

We are most grateful to our colleagues, Professor Dietrich Niethammer of Tübingen, who is a doctor of medicine, and Professor Albin Eser of Freiburg, who is a doctor of law, for joining our discussion and adding their critical reflections. Our plea aims to do two things: first, to introduce a necessary change of awareness in a frontier area which many people find oppressive. Secondly, to lift the discussion to another ethical level. Here we are moved by the hope that the question of our responsibility for our own dying can be discussed afresh in a sober, dignified and morally serious way – without dogmatism and without fundamentalist reasoning. The problem is too important to be left to the decisions of specialists. We are aware how tabu the question is, and of course expect this plea for active help in dying to come up against resistance in many places. But perhaps it will also command assent among all those who want to find a new way of dealing with the last great question of any human life: in the awareness that humane self-determination, as the presupposition for an existence which is trustworthy and sets an example in both the social and the personal sphere, may not end when it comes to the issue of dying. 'Human dignity is inviolable': this first clause of the constitution also applies to our dying, and it should be our lifelong task to see that this happens in a humane way.

Tübingen, December 1994   Walter Jens   Hans Küng

A Dignified Dying

Hans Küng

We shall hardly be able to avoid misunderstanding, the fatal misunderstanding that here two men are beginning to reflect in public about dying now that they themselves have unmistakably grown old and cannot exclude the possibility that in the foreseeable future death will be knocking on their own doors. *Emeriti morituri vos salutant* . . . Emeritus professors who are about to die salute you! So are we hastily meditating on death while there is still time, before the end comes? Are we hastily meditating once more on being ill, on dying, on death, before we become senile and are possibly no longer in a position to reflect?

This misunderstanding could not be more fatal. For Walter Jens and I have been colleaagues now for more than thirty years and friends for more than twenty, and for us reflecting on death has never been a matter of age but a question at the centre of our lives, which have often been so hectic, so intellectually strenuous and so full of struggle. It is a question which has dogged us since we got to know each other:
– How are things today? How will they be tomorrow? What is it like to grow old?
– What does it mean to know that we are mortal and have to die?
– Are we afraid of death or just afraid of dying?
– How would we like to die if we could have a hand in it? Can we have a hand in it, may we have a hand in it, may we even decide to die? But who can decide to die? There are so many who have nothing to decide, either in living or in dying.

Undignified dying

We are both convinced, and this is so to speak the presupposition of our reflections, that millions upon millions of people have no choice, do not even have the slightest chance, of dying a dignified death. Every day the media show us pictures of people, often masses of people, who have been tortured to death and driven to death, in war and in flight, through natural catastrophes, famine and epidemics. They die an undignified death, literally on the rack, their limbs stretched out stiff, as wretched as stray dogs.

Think of all the things that would have to be done to avoid or at least to stem such undignified dying, to the degree that it is the fault of human beings. Think of all the things that would have to be done to ensure a better, more dignified life, or at least basic survival for these people, whose life is often worse than a dog's life. For without dignified living there can be no dignified dying. And conversely, even under the conditions of an affluent society, dignified dying is not something that can be taken for granted. Dignified dying is an undeserved opportunity, a great gift: the great gift. However, it is also a great task.

For we are both also convinced that there is more to dignified dying than social conditions. Dignified dying also depends on the way in which we have dealt with the question of death from the midst of life. For what distinguishes us human beings from stray dogs is that we can know that we are mortal. And though molecular biologists, who have been able to extend the lives of mice by around thirty per cent, claim that in theory, by cutting down our calorie intake, many of us could live to be 110 years old, what's the use? We must die one day. And we alone among all human beings are aware of our mortality. This too, rightly understood, is a great gift, though this too – and here again is the other side – is a great task.

But what does a dignified way of dealing with dying mean? It does not mean simply understanding dying as a final phase of life with which one grapples when death is insistently at the door. Rather, it is a matter of understanding dying as a dimension of life which helps to determine all the phases and all the decisions of life. Martin Heidegger quotes the 'Bohemian ploughman's' remark, 'As soon as man comes to life, he is at once old enough to die,'[1] to define human existence as being towards death. We are to live constantly in sober remembrance of the fact that as a rule we are given a good deal of time for living, but at some point we must depart, we must let go. We are finite beings. It is important to acquire a spirituality of *memento mori*, which is not to stand as a gloomy threat over all of life or at the end of life, but which makes another, perhaps even serene, basic attitude possible in the midst of life – for life. Those who do not suppress their death, but consciously accept it, live differently. Those who do not postpone dealing with their own dying until their 'deathbeds', but practise it in the midst of life, have a different basic attitude to life. Even today in some hospitals people still speak of death only in whispers. Here I want to make a contribution to the practice of a conscious attitude to dying. And doesn't the present social situation in particular require us to talk of dying and of death, to a certain degree contrary to the facts?

Experiencing life – and death?

If we follow the most recent sociology of contemporary culture produced by Gerhard Schulze in 1993 under the title *The Experience Society*, we have to note three phases of development in postwar Germany. The first phase of a restored industrial society, between 1945–1968, was dominated by the question of survival and work, which not least brought relief from the moral topics of zero hour, and after National Socialism created a new meaning in life: 'The religious interest of the population was matched by a zeal for work which was often elevated into a philosophy of life. Work brought not only money but also a guaranteed meaning in life as ethical capital.'[2] Furthermore, people had seen enough dead bodies; now they were intent on life, intent on living better lives than their comrades, relatives and acquaintances who had been killed by bullets, bombs, fires and collapsing buildings.

After very modest beginnings on the experience market of supply and demand in the postwar period, during the course of the 1960s a second phase developed. This was a transitional phase of cultural conflict, in which not least age played a great role: the primacy of youth, established in the student revolts and taken up in the quest for eternal youth, favoured reflection on

dying even less than the concentration on work which preceded
it. Now there was a 'tremendous thrust towards aestheticizing'
which aimed at a life whose every aspect was beautiful, attractive,
interesting, fascinating, aesthetically pleasant, so that people
found their satisfaction, their fulfilment, indeed their happiness in
it: 'Consumer motivation with an inner orientation celebrated its
triumph here. Equipped with ever higher potential demands for
experience – time, money, mobility, equipment – consumers
discovered the possibility of aestheticizing the whole of everyday
life. The public conquered unlimited areas: listening to music,
travelling, buying clothes, eating and drinking, sexuality, dance,
going out in the evening, and so on. The new wealth of experience
could still prove fascinating.'[3] However, criticism of the
tremendous 'intensification of the consumption of experience by
better exploitation of the capacity for experience among those
demanding it' and the resultant depersonalization soon also
developed, criticism of 'commerce' and 'consumption'. According to Schulze, the magic words of the conflictual phase of this
politics of culture were 'creativity', 'fulfilment', 'autonomy',
'identity', 'do it yourself', 'activation', 'animation'. But precisely
because of this the 'orientation on experience' increasingly took
the side of the critics of society. There developed what today, in a
third phase of the post-war development during the 1980s and
1990s, is called the 'experience society'.

What characterizes this experience society? It is a society in
which experience has often become an end in itself, and having
the experience of something – from a new coat to a new car – is
more important than the usefulness of the item. What I enjoy,
what I like, what gives me pleasure, what drives away boredom,
what helps towards success, is permissible. In this society the
experience market has become a dominant sphere of daily life in
which the supply has become increasingly refined and at the same
time the demand has become increasingly routine: 'Everything
has been tried, not only the established products but also,
paradoxical though it may sound, the innovative ones as well.
The public has become accustomed to the new. Once replacement
has been elevated to a principle, it imperceptibly becomes
repetition. With indifference the public registers the incessant

stream of mutations of experience on offer: fashions and trends, information, product changes, gimmicks offering new experiences, innovative programmes in the electronic media, new releases for the charts in the music world and new magazines, the last word in new areas of tourism, bold new productions in the theatre, revolutionary stylistic changes, provocative scandals, and so on.'[4] There is an unprecedented concentration on experience in everyday life. However, 'the further the principle of cumulation is driven, the more the motive of longing for the beautiful turns into the motive of avoiding boredom'.[5]

In a society in which experience is brought into the centre and the whole of life is conceived of as a project of experience, of what interest is that dimension of dying, of death, which is so remote, alien, to be avoided in everyday life? Now it represents the absolute, final end of all experience that cannot be avoided by any manipulation or suggestion of experience. While the participants in such an experience society, retiring at an increasingly earlier age, but capable of work and entertainment for longer and longer, may 'amuse themselves to death',[6] they do not talk of death itself. Dying is not a topic. Dying and death are suppressed from the 'experience society'. They are disruptive factors which people attempt to exclude. And though they may sometimes say, 'I would die rather than experience such a performance, such a holiday trip, such a marriage again', they do not mean it seriously; usually they soon attempt something new.

Only in one respect has dying been able to arouse the intense interest of the experience society, and this is not surprising: dying itself as an experience, the experiences of those who have died and have been brought back from death. What sort of an experience is this?

The experience of dying

Never in almost thirty-five years at the university have I seen such tremendous public interest as when I invited Elisabeth Kübler-Ross to come to Tübingen for a lecture and discussion. This professor of psychiatry, who initially was regarded with mistrust by some doctors and theologians, is the author of a book *On*

Death and Dying.[7] As is well known, she and others like
Raymond A. Moody[8] have collected experiences of dying from
those who have been 'medically dead'. In many ways these
experiences show striking similarities: dying people (cancer
victims, accident victims, those who have drowned, been frozen
to death or fallen from great heights) can hear the doctor
declaring them dead, experience a movement through a long dark
tunnel, experience leaving their own bodies, encounter already
dead relatives and friends, and even a light-being emanating love
and warmth, calling for an evaluation of life as a whole. The most
important stages of life go past in a lightning retrospect as though
in a panorama: one approaches a kind of barrier or limit,
evidently the dividing wall between earthly life and the life which
follows . . . And then there is a return to earth again, but with
overwhelming feelings of joy, love and peace.

Thus far the phenomena may be taken to be confirmed. But
what conclusions are to be drawn from them? Not only
psychological, but also philosophical and theological? First of all
it has to be said that such experiences are evidently human
experiences, and are symptoms of a dignified dying which we
should neither deny nor despise. They have taken the excessive
fears of dying from countless people and given them the hope that
dying, which many look to with sorrow, even with fear and
trembling, may not be as full of anxiety in the very last phase –
perhaps – as is often feared. It is thanks to the numerous doctors
who have made a study of death, experts in thanatology, that the
tabu of the problem of death has been broken, not least in medicine
itself, and more scientific attention has been paid to dying.

A second point should be added immediately. Something that
Elisabeth Kübler-Ross has observed in more than two thousand
terminally ill patients is a considerable help in practising a
dignified dying: the fact that, where men and women are given
time, there are several stages of dying, which differ widely
depending on the individual and by no means always take place in
the same order. Such patients, whether or not they have religious
affiliations, react in a first phase with shock and unbelief, which
can last seconds or months. Then follows phase 2, anger,
annoyance, resentment and envy, often directed at the nursing

staff or at relatives. If these accept it without offence, the transition towards phase 3, negotiations over prolonging life, is easier. This often leads rapidly to phase 4, depression about the hopeless situation. Only after that – with or without the help of others – does the final phase 5 come: final acceptance, assent and surrender, in short the capacity to let go of all ties – an indication of the death which is soon to come.

Beyond question these insights into the stages of dying have helped many doctors and nurses, and also many relatives, not just to look on a person's dying with spiritual helplessness and confusion, but to offer human support for it, in tune with the changing moods of the terminally ill, so that in the interpersonal dimension, too, theirs can be a dignified dying. Here one of the most important insights of Kübler-Ross seems to me to be that the sick person very often traces the advent of death by psychological and physical signals which are unknown to us, and that we only make the leave-taking more difficult if in a well-meaning way we attempt to talk the person concerned out of dying. Perhaps this is one of the reasons why some of those who are terminally ill prefer to say how they feel to the nurses rather than to their relatives, who may be protesting and lamenting, indeed why individuals even want to die alone, or die shortly after relatives have left the room.

However, a third point must now be made equally clearly: these experiences of dying tell us nothing about a life after death – no matter what doctors or theologians may have inferred from them. There are at least three reasons why this is so.

1. Similar phenomena can also be noted in other special psychological states – in dreams, in schizophrenia, in intoxication by hallucinogens (LSD, mescalin, etc.) and in suggestion – which have nothing whatever to do with a 'beyond' or an 'other world'.[9]

2. It has been observed that as well as a kind of dying which is full of joy and light, there can also be quite painful and anxious forms of dying, for example with poisonings.[10]

3. A scientific medical explanation of these phenomena within the framework of the existing laws of nature certainly cannot be ruled out: isn't there projection and combination here, as also with the appearance of familiar figures in dreams? Can't one even see oneself in a dream? And cannot perhaps the central nervous

system at the particular point of extreme pressure, with febrile intensity and rapidity, produce images of the past and the future, euphoric feelings, extraordinary stimuli of light, simple or complex visions – something like a last 'substitute taking breath' of the dying brain, just as the fire flickers a last time before finally collapsing?

But the real reason why these experiences of dying have nothing to do with another world, a sphere beyond the senses, has not yet been mentioned. Reflection which takes us beyond dying is urgently necessary. Why do the experiences of dying prove nothing about a life after death? The real reason is as simple as it is illuminating: because these dying people did not really die; they were not definitively dead. But this fact provokes the question: mustn't what we call 'death' be completely redefined?

What is death?

Those who have made studies of death explain that people in whom experiences of dying could be verified had been 'medically dead'. What does that mean? It means that they were in a state in which while breathing, heartbeat, brain reaction, perhaps even the brainstem activity that can be detected only by an electro-encephalogram had stopped ('zero line EGG'), revival – say through artifical respiration or heart massage – was still possible. In normal cases, such reanimation must take place within five minutes if the brain is not to be irreparably damaged by a lack of oxygen, but in extreme cases like hyupothermia the period can be up to thirty minutes. So these patients were 'medically' and only medically dead.

At the same time this means that such people were not biologically dead. For to be biologically dead means that at least the brain (in contrast, perhaps, to the kidneys, which can still be transplanted) has completely and irrevocably ceased to function and can no longer be revived. Biological death is not just an organic death or a partial death but brain death ('central death'), and finally the death of the whole organism ('total death'). Only someone who has died not only medically but biologically has experienced final, universal death, and that is the irrevocable loss of the functions of life with consequential decay of all organs and tissues.

Even those who have researched into death do not dispute that someone who has had experiences of dying and can subsequently report them has not gone through the phase of death but through a particular phase of life: possibly the last few minutes and seconds between 'medical' death and biological death. Such a person stood on the threshold of death but nowhere crossed it. He or she had come very close indeed to the great 'exit' door, but did not see what lies behind it. No dead person has ever been able to report what it was like 'out there', where death really leads. Therefore such experiences of dying do not prove anything about a possible life after death. Or isn't it the other way round? Hasn't it been proved, at least indirectly, that there is nothing beyond life, that with death it is all over?

Is it all over with death?

From a philosophical perspective, the reason why not only experiences of dying prove nothing about a life after death, but our reason cannot prove anything at all here, lies in a permanently valid insight of Immanuel Kant, that no conclusive knowledge can be gained about a reality which is not in space and time and thus is not the object of our perception. Proofs for a life after death thus not only fail but are theoretically impossible: 'All those conclusions of ours which profess to lead us beyond the field of possible experience,' says Kant, are 'deceptive and without foundation.'[11] Indeed, our reason spreads its wings in vain, trying by the power of thought to get beyond the world of phenomena and come upon an eternal life. And not only do the trees not grow up to heaven; even the skyscrapers we plan and build so boldly fail to do so. At best they scrape the sky, but they cannot open the heavens.

So is it clear that with death all is over? No, the opposite has not been proved either. And according to the selfsame Kant, all the arguments of a trivial or dialectical materialism which seek to prove that all is up with death fail for precisely the same reason: the counter-proofs against an eternal life also transcend the horizon of our experience. 'For from what source could we, through a purely speculative employment of reason, derive the insight that there is no supreme being as the ultimate ground of all things?'[12] Those who concede that they cannot look behind the great portal may not logically conclude that there is nothing behind it either. Like experiences of dying, so too philosophical arguments do not decide the question where the dying go: whether into a comfortless dark or into a friendly eternal light; into a nothingness or into a new being. And if research into dying has achieved anything, it is this: that the question of a life after death, which since the nineteenth century has often been dismissed with allegedly scientific and medical arguments, is today once again an open question even for doctors as doctors.

But doesn't this also mean that in practice the question 'What comes after death?' has become one on which it is almost impossible to decide? According to Kant, at any rate, no. The question here is not one of 'pure', theoretical, scientific reason but one of practical reason; not of science but of morality. And Kant's second moral postulate – alongside that of human freedom – is the immortality of the soul: in their lives, human beings can at best achieve virtue but not holiness, only good and not perfection, yet they stand under the unconditional imperative 'You should', which therefore requires infinite human progress. Human beings may finally be happy, infinitely happy, blissful. But bliss can be fulfilled only by the 'supreme good', by God.

As I have said, none of this can be proved, but according to Kant it can be postulated for the sake of morality. 'God and eternity with their awful majesty' – this is Kant's Calvinistic legacy – could not 'stand unceasingly before our eyes'.[13] Therefore Kant affirms the mystery, as he maintains it in a posthumously published note: 'It is good for us not to know but to believe that there is a God.'[14]

But today of course Feuerbach and Freud are summoned against Kant. 'God' and eternal life are only a projection, a fiction, illusion, wishful thinking.

Just wishful thinking?

My reply is, 'Of course, it is also always "wishful thinking".' What authority could really forbid me to wish that everything were not over with death? This is even more than just wishful thinking; it is wishful being: human beings are undeniably wishful beings, infinite beings with infinite longing who endlessly seek the imperfect, unfinished, unfulfilled; who find and seek again, know and doubt again, enjoy and remain unsatisfied even in their enjoyment. 'For all joy wants eternity, wants deep, deep eternity,' as Friedrich Nietzsche remarked.[15] And where is deep, deep eternity to be found?

What demonstrates more than our present-day affluent society, whose members retire earlier and earlier but are capable ∨ of work and enjoyment for longer and longer, that even today no affluence in the world is capable of satisfying men and women? This affluent society offers everything, and parades it in its great advertising campaigns featuring bright smiling faces. And are we happier than former generations, as we are offered ever bigger and better products, from cars, computers and stereo systems to household equipment and sports clothes? As research into satisfaction has shown, human beings are subjectively satisfied only provisionally, because time and again even newer and better offers overtrump the earlier ones and create a desire for new experiences. To quote Gerhard Schulze once more, the very orientation of our experience society on experience 'becomes the habitualized hunger which no longer allows any satisfaction': 'At the moment of fulfilment the question "What next?" already arises, so that satisfaction no longer stops anywhere, because the quest for satisfaction has become a habit.' And the sociologist adds: 'Weekends and holidays, but also relationships with partners, jobs and other spheres of life are subjected to a pressure of expectation which engenders disappointments. The more unconditional experiences are made *the* meaning of life, the greater the anxiety about missing out on experiences . . . Anxiety about boredom is linked with anxiety about missing something.'[16]

Indeed human beings are restless, always on the way, constantly reaching out for the other and the new. The author of *The Principle of Hope*, Ernst Bloch, was not the first to recognize this. As is well known, the theme of the *cor inquietum*, the 'restless heart', already appears with the first great psychologist of antiquity, the theologian Augustine. However, for him this infinite human longing does not run out into emptiness. For 'Our heart is restless,' he says, 'until it rests in' – and here it is no longer so easy to follow him – 'you . . . O Lord.'[17] But Ernst Bloch, too, more critical than other atheists, out of curiosity maintained to the end a *'peut-être'*, a 'perhaps', about a life after death and was fond of quoting the words of the dying Rabelais: 'So I'm going to see the great Perhaps.'[18] Thus the constantly repeated argument that to hope for more beyond this life is wishful thinking may be shelved today. It has been seen through: all the indisputable influence of conscious and unconscious depth-psychological factors on belief in an eternal life does not determine whether or not there is eternal life. Even Freud could not avoid conceding at the end of his critical work on religion the possibility of the existence of God and a life beyond: 'It would splendid if . . .'[19] For even if it cannot be proved, the wish for eternal life could be matched by a real eternal life, and the human urge for the infinite could be matched by a real Infinite.

Where does that leave us? If the evidence is lacking, so too is the pressure; we make the happy discovery that we have complete freedom. That there is a life after death is simply a matter of trust – very much in line with Kant, but combining both pure and practical reason, critical rationality and enlightened credibility. However, this is not a blind trust. This trust is not just a theoretical affair, nor is it simply a matter of irrational feelings and emotional moods. Rather, it is a practical, existential, basic human attitude which is rationally quite responsible. In other words, it is reasonable trust. That means that it is a trust (with a structure like love) which, while it cannot be proved rationally (there are no rational proofs), does have its reasons (it is a reasonable trust).

Reasons? Yes, I passionately want my life, which has made sense through all the suffering and fighting in which I have been involved, not to end in a meaningless absurd death. I want my family and friends not to go into nothingness when they die. I want not to remain speechless in death and in the grave. And I find the contrary hardly rational. Indeed, it seems to me that like Dostoyevsky's Ivan Karamazov, one would have to hand back one's entrance ticket to this world if in the end of the day there were no justice, and the exploiters could triumph definitively over the poor, the murderers of children triumph definitively over the children they had murdered. My reason would find it intolerable if those who had been trampled on and tortured, those who had had to lead a dog's life, did not finally come into their own and find happiness. And I am not alone in this conviction. There is a testimony to it which is not to be despised, diachronic and synchronic, through all times and all spaces.

The great mystery of death

The religions have always prepared people for dying. And the graves of Stone Age people and the tremendous tombs of the Egyptians bear witness to belief in a life after death. Down to the present day, all the great religions agree that the life which human beings usually lead is an unreal one. Men and women are not free, are not really themselves. In other words, the present status of human beings is unsatisfactory, full of suffering, unhappy. Why? Because human beings have to live lives that are separated, alienated from that hidden, supreme, Ultimate Reality which is their true home, which constitutes their real freedom, represents their real identity, and which they call the Unconditional, the Inexpressible, the Absolute, the Deity, God, or whatever. The meaning of life is achieved in its end. Death is the great mystery: not a final end but a consummation.

Here the issue is not simply, say, the belief of Christians (as of Jews and Muslims) in a resurrection, which today we may no longer understand in a naively physiological way as a revival of corpses – as though the creator of the world were dependent on the elements of this body, and Paul had not already spoken of a *soma pneumatikon*, a spiritual corporeality. Resurrection means a completely other life, bursting out of the dimensions of space and time, in the invisible, incomprehensible divine sphere which is symbolically called 'heaven'.

We must also take into consideration – to mention only the extreme opposite to the prophetic religions – the Buddhist conviction of a 'Nirvana', of a 'quenching', i.e. of a final state without suffering, greed, hatred and blindness, which is understood by very few Buddhists indeed as total and utter extinction. Rather, following some passages in the old Buddhist canon,[20] Nirvana is spoken of as 'a transcendent "metaphysical" place or essence elevated above all the conditions of phenomenal existence, the deathless place (*amritam padam*), that which has not come into being, has not become and has not been caused'. As L. Schmithausen, an expert of Buddhism, puts it: 'The mode of being of the redeemed is an unfathomable, incomprehensible state, and this state is occasionally even described as joyful.'[21]

Both Christianity and Buddhism therefore know an ultimately indescribable 'other shore', another dimension, a transcendent reality, the true reality, of which one can speak only in images. Despite all the differences there is no mistaking a convergence of ideas.

– Certainly in general Buddhists guard against speaking of the ongoing existence of the individual in Nirvana. Yet they make so many positive statements about a final state without suffering that some correspondence with the Christian notion of an 'eternal' life cannot be ruled out *a priori*.

– Christians for their part certainly emphasize that the notion of an 'eternal life' includes an ongoing existence of the human person. But they remain quite aware that their statements about 'eternal life' are only images of the unimaginable and that finite personhood loses all the limitations of the finite in the dimension of the infinite, beyond time and space.

A continuity in discontinuity: if we are to use an image for this, then probably it should be not so much that of the drop of water dissolving in the ocean (even according to the Buddhist view, human beings are more than drops of water) as perhaps that of the pupa which slips out of the cocoon and becomes a butterfly. It is the image of delimitation, liberation and redemption for a free existence which is no longer bound to 'earthly', temporal dimensions but is released into 'heavenly', eternal dimensions. The question which is often asked, whether we shall see our loved ones again, can be answered only by noting both the individual and the more-than-individual character of the final state where there is no suffering. Certainly our loved ones will be the same finite persons, but in quite another dimension, infinite in the real dimension – and this is unimaginable, something that no human eye has seen nor ear heard.

According to such a Christian idea, which is also Jewish and Muslim, in death human beings do not die into nothingness. Rather, they are taken up into that incomprehensible and ineffable last and first reality which is pure spirituality beyond space and time: the eternal, most real reality. There is a transformation through new creation and an eternal hiddenness in God. 'God' is then not only 'in all things' but 'all in all' (I Corinthians 15.28). I ask myself whether such a view of death cannot also change, indeed illuminate, the human view of dying.

Another attitude to dying

Of course it should not be forgotten for a moment that the 'godless' person, the atheist or agnostic who regards death as an inexplicable, unfathomable brute fact, can die bravely and with serenity. On the other hand, there is no mistaking the fact that this unfathomable bane of modern life has taken on an oppressive weight of its own since the rise of atheism – as can be seen from Feuerbach to Jean-Paul Sartre – often characterized by utter comfortlessness. So I can understand how some people who believe that they are dying into nothingness may attempt to postpone the moment of death as long as possible, even if they are not necessarily afraid of dying.

Death should be fought against with every means, but can it ultimately be destroyed? In the midst of the French Revolution, the last philosopher of the Enlightenment, Antoine de Condorcet, proclaimed in his *Outline of a Historical Account of the Progress of the Human Spirit*[22] an abolition or at least a considerable postponement of death as the ultimate goal of the modern development. That this bold revolutionary and visionary, under suspicion and arrested as an opponent of Robespierre, had to die in a revolutionary prison, of a stroke or perhaps one of the poison pills which his friend Cabanis had been handing out to those who were being persecuted, was as unwelcome a counter-argument to this utopia as the death of Condorcet's Tübingen translator Ernst Ludwig Posselt, who, when he was iimplicated in a high treason trial, finally hurled himself to his death from a window in Heidelberg.[23]

No, those who believe in God should not dispute that unbelievers, too, can die bravely. But conversely, unbelievers should not deny that because of their belief in God as the last reality, believers can adopt a different attitude to dying. For trusting in a power which embraces all men and women, with which human beings enter into a relationship of a totally different character when all the other relationships to people and things break off, those who are terminally ill need not anxiously cling on to this life as their last resort. Rather, in great freedom, serenity and comfort they may rely on an ultimate Reality. They know that the fight for health is meaningful as long as healing is possible, but that a fight against death at any price is nonsensical: it is a help which becomes a torment. Moreover doctors who, always confronted with their own mortality, nevertheless believe in an ultimate reality, will not see death as their deadly enemy and make victory over death a question of prestige. In the end they will accept and endure their own helplessness, and will deal sensitively with death, not avoiding it when they can no longer fight against it. In this way they will be capable of supporting the dying to the end and will not go away the moment death comes. Therefore:

Real human support until death

It cannot be emphasized enough how important for incurable illnesses all human care to the end is: the human care of doctors and nurses, which health insurance schemes cannot calculate and patients cannot pay for, but which is more precious than many expensive drugs. Maximum care, minimal therapy: this is usually given as the rule for present-day care of the dying, and an experienced nurse of terminal patients wrote to me: 'First make the bed, then pray; pastoral care includes physical care.'

Highly technological medicine in particular, which provides therapy through apparatuses, must not lead to the terminally ill being left alone. The perfect clinic must not become a mere service station with maximal biochemical care and at the same time minimal human care. Happily, today more and more doctors and nurses are making sure, in view of the danger of depersonalization in our hospitals, that the dominance of apparatus and medicine which is a threat everywhere is stopped by a new dominance of the human person. A patient-orientated doctor knows that men and women are helped only by a total care which embraces both body and soul, and that a humane climate in the clinic and above all human conversation is important to the end. Despite all the necessary therapeutical distance and unavoidable matter-of-factness, sensitivity and caring humanity are always important. Only in this way can the terminally ill be told responsibly, as far as they can take it, what their real situation is, without being thrown into panic. Only in this way can dying be made easier rather than more difficult for them.

At the same time, however, human care and concern are needed for family and friends, who are lovingly looking after the most seriously ill as far as they can and who, when the time has come, will help them to sort out their family, financial and religious affairs. If they know how operations, pain, radiation and chemotherapy can change people, and understand the different phases of dying – shock, rebellion, doubt, negotiation and depression – then they will make the sick person's waiting for death easier. Today's care of the body, which is usually as good as can be, does not of itself help the tortured soul. Patiently to give time to the terminally ill is perhaps the greatest and last gift: time to listen to their uncertainties, worries and anxieties, to give a bit of comfort, and also to say a prayer with them. Today we know how well in some circumstances a person who is terminally ill and can no longer speak can still hear, how much bodily contact can provide spiritual security, even for those who can no longer move. Isn't this concrete form of human support also part of a dignified dying?

Of course here human beings should not be asked to do the impossible. Every form of care has its limits. Doctors and nurses have other duties. Families and friends cannot simply devote themselves exclusively to the care of the seriously ill. They may have jobs to do. But what is to be done when the doctors have done what they can, when they declare medical treatment under their supervision at an end and ask the family to take the sick person home? Most people certainly want to spend the last phase of their life at home, but in many cases this in particular is impossible in practice. Because of the enormity of the burden, members of the family are afraid that it will prove too much. The break-up of the wider family and single existence have changed many things. If the members of the family have jobs, some kind of home care service can help, or the daily visit of a district nurse who can wash or inject the sick. But if this is not possible, sending the sick person to an old peoples' home or a nursing home will be unavoidable.

But even a 'nice single room' will not in itself be a guarantee of a dignified dying for the terminally ill who have been told that medical care for them is at an end. And if we realize that a hospital cannot be a hospice, we will have to give even more encouragement to the efforts of those who are concerned for a dignified dying in a hospice where the terminally ill are lovingly cared for to the end by a specially trained professional personnel, who can cope with the emotional burdens associated with their work. Now that nursing assurance has been approved by the German parliament, it may be easier for the hospice movement originating in America and England to found hospices in Germany as well. Here at present we have around a hundred hospices, each with between ten and fifteen places. In them expensive medical apparatus is not used; life is not artificially prolonged, but dying is made as tolerable as possible with the use of painkillers: life is conscious to the end.[24]

But there is no overlooking the fact that today there are more people than before – whether at home, in hospital or in a hospice – who can no longer bear their already destroyed life, whose indescribable pain is not relieved even by the strongest sedatives of palliative therapy. They do not want to be made unconscious by means of psychotropic drugs or morphine and so be deprived of dialogue with family and friends. They want to say good-bye with a clear consciousness and die. And as they cannot die, they want effective help towards dying a dignified death. Today's discussion, some of which is highly emotional, is about what kind of help in dying in a humane, dignified and therefore moral way is possible.

Uncontroversial help in dying

I need not speak here of the growing problems which the tremendous extension of human life poses both to individuals and to society. As the German Federal Office of Statistics reported in May 1994, already one in five of the population of Germany is over sixty, and in twenty-five years one in four will have passed this mark; today 3.8% of all Germans belong in the category of the very old, being more than eighty years old. I need not spell out the economic and social effects of this, especially for provision for old age by social security and the broadening of the age pyramid from the base upwards, because fewer and fewer young people have to care for more and more older people. The gigantic state obligation can make one anxious and uneasy.

But there is one tricky topic that I cannot pass over. Increasingly, old people and whole groups often find that the artificial extension of life is not a benefit but a burden. So they proclaim their right to a 'natural death' and call for a change in legislation about active help in dying, or euthanasia. A referendum in the state of Washington in 1991, in which 46% voted for the legalization of voluntary death for the terminally ill with the assistance of a doctor, is a pointer for Europe.

It is well known that especially in the Netherlands, some things are tolerated which are forbidden in Germany. I must of course leave medical and legal casuistry to the specialists of both disciplines, and I gladly also leave detailed questions of medical ethics to professionals who have special qualifications in that area. But the casuistic questions will be decided in the light of general basic philosophical and theological positions, and on these I can and must comment as a theologian. So I shall first make a few brief remarks about what is today regarded as uncontroversial in the question of help in dying.

1. There is no dispute over the moral reprehensibility of any form of compulsory euthanasia which advocates pseudo-help in dying or pseudo-euthanasia. Since the mass murder of Jews, gypsies and slaves who were alleged to be 'unfit to live', since the forcible killing of physically or mentally ill men and women (it is estimated that on the basis of a secret decree of Adolf Hitler, from 1 September 1939 to August 1941 between 60,000 and 80,000 people were killed in special 'killing institutions'), since all these abominable atrocities against human dignity, there is no disputing the fact that this form of compulsory 'euthanasia' on state orders is nothing short of cold-blooded murder. And the major international declarations by doctors since the Second World War make it clear that compulsory euthanasia is unthinkable and an offence against basic human rights. In view of these crimes, the very phrase 'unfit to live' should not pass anyone's lips.[25]

The word 'euthanasia' is not the same. It is understandable that since the Hitler period this term, too, has largely been avoided in Germany. But in Graeco-Roman antiquity this old word originally meant 'good dying', a 'beautiful', i.e. a good, quick, easy, painless death. And *'euthanasia medica'* was first recognized as a task of doctors by Francis Bacon at the beginning of the sixteenth century: the relief of pain in dying. The word euthanasia is still used all over the world in this positive or neutral sense. So in Germany, too, this word must not remain stigmatized once and for all.

2. There is no dispute over the ethical responsibility of authentic help in dying or euthanasia which does not shorten life. In it, doctors limit themselves to providing pain-killers or sedatives. And it is part of a dignified dying today that a patient's bodily suffering should be reduced to a tolerable level and that the human psyche should also be supported by psychotropic drugs in coping emotionally with the last phase of life. Such help in dying is legally beyond reproach, ethically responsible and medically necessary. Sustaining life must go hand in hand with relieving

suffering and supporting freedom.[26] Saving life may not become a postponement of dying.

3. Finally, there is no disputing the ethical responsibility of passive help in dying or euthanasia which shortens life as a side-effect: i.e. indirect help in dying by stopping artificial prolongation of life. That no extraordinary means need be applied in sustaining life is a principle of classical moral theology. So no patient is ethically obliged in any situation to accept any possible therapy or operation to prolong life. It is not for the doctor but for the patient to decide, after being given relevant information, whether in a particular case to undergo yet another operation and therefore die later but possibly more painfully, or not to undergo it, so as to die earlier, but also more easily. It is the right of the sick person to decide freely about medical clinical care. No doctor has an obligation to strive for prolongation of life at any price and to treat complications which may arise in a more long-drawn out process of dying. No doctor need continue a particular therapy endlessly; doctors may allow patients to die a 'natural' death, even if this takes place earlier because medical treatment is broken off or there is no intervention.[27] All this is indeed help in dying in which the doctor remains passive and the shortening of life happens indirectly, and there is no longer any dispute over this passive or indirect help in dying among doctors, lawyers and theologians. There is one important result: evidently even according to conservative Christian doctrine, patients are not intervening in the exclusive rights of the creator in making a personal decision about the hour or day of their death in this way.[28]

However, there is vigorous dispute over active help in dying, active euthanasia, which leads directly to the shortening of life, 'mercy-killing'.[29]

Controversial help in dying: 'mercy-killing'

For a long time the rejection of any active help in dying was largely a matter of course; and in some states like England and France help towards voluntary death, even if this was the result of an unambiguous wish, was punishable under the law (up to fourteen years in prison). But we cannot avoid noting that more and more people and organizations (associations for voluntary euthanasia, 'Exit' organizations) are calling for the legalization of voluntarily requested 'mercy-killing' by a doctor who is prepared to help. The first World Conference of these 'Right to Die Societies' took place in 1976. It passed a 'Tokyo Declaration' with the following programmatic statements: 1. All persons should decide about their own life and death; 2. Advance directives ('living wills') are to be recognized as a human right. 3. They must be recognized as legal documents. At that time there were eight such national organizations for help in dying; today there are already thirty, twenty-five of which issue advance directives which are also recognized by law in some countries; twelve organizations also have a system of personally empowered permanent legal support for medical care which is activated when a seriously ill patient is no longer in a position to make decisions ('The Durable Power of Attorney for Health Cases').

The question of active help in dying understandably stirs up deep emotions on all sides. And the journalistic exploitation of such wishes to die by individual doctors – the messianic campaign of a euthanasia doctor in the state of Michigan which has become known world–wide, often without precise knowledge of the patient and his or her illness, or the shameful way in which the former president of the 'German Society for Humane Dying' sold cyanide – have seriously damaged the concerns of those who support responsible active help in dying. But in my view they call even more for legal regulation appropriate to the situation. Here it is no help, especially in Germany, to make rational discussion of active help in dying tabu with references to the Nazi period and to compare all those who seek to produce more sophisticated arguments to Nazi murderers. It is wrong simply to identify any form of active help in dying with 'murder', as though this were not an 'act of mercy' quite voluntarily asked for by the person concerned, but an act of violence inflicted against the patient's will. Many euthanasia organizations even have the term 'voluntary' in their titles. Moreover, not a single Exit organization calls for the legalization of active help in dying without at the same time calling for compulsory medical controlling authorities.

In every case there has to be a legally authenticated and completely voluntary declaration on the part of the person concerned, who himself or herself specifies the precise conditions of their dying – wider or narrower: euthanasia either only in the case of an incurable disease leading to death or also in the case of a bodily ailment which is not fatal but severe and painful (difficulty in breathing); or finally also in the case of severe or irreparable brain damage or illness.

And here the whole dispute now comes to a head: is it also part of a dignified dying for people to be able to decide as far as possible the time and manner of their deaths? In the Christian view, do human beings have the right to control whether or not they shall live? It should be noted that I am not putting this question in connection with psychologically or physically healthy people, but in connection with the seriously ill who are ready to die. A dozen years ago, when I first spoke at this university about questions of dying, I was moved by the concern that in offering such reflections I might lead some people to false conclusions. I still am today. Perhaps there is someone who has simply grown tired of life, whose first love has fallen apart or whose study or professional career has collapsed, and who now despairs of life. Breaking off the great experiment of life when it has not even properly begun? Without the experience that brave endurance of suffering can make people more human and more mature? No, such suicide remains irresponsible and morally illegitimate for Christians.

So here I am speaking exclusively about the cases of people who (whether older or younger) are at the end of their lives, and who thus are going irreversibly towards their deaths (for instance with inoperable cancer or the last stage of Aids). May such people decide about their lives at this point? Is there a right to self-determination – which is also responsible in a Christian way – in dying as in living? May the doctor also be asked for active help in dying? May a doctor offer such help?

Active help in dying? Why not? That so far has been the comment of all non-Christian or non-religious supporters. Human beings have this right on the basis of their autonomous control of themselves, and the liberal constitutional state has to make the perception of this right possible by legislation and jurisprudence. If the churches, as an ideological minority, take a different view, they have not to attempt to supervise other men and women. Anyone who so wishes should be able, with foresight, to put a stop to the delaying measures of technical medicine by an advance directive which he or she has drafted personally. Such a directive should also be legally binding on doctors, unless there are demonstrable reasons why it no longer corresponds to the current desire of the patient. At the same time the legalization of voluntary active help in dying should be fought for. It is not the doctor who is the lord of life and death, but only the individual concerned, who may claim his or her right from the doctor.

Active help in dying? Not at all, has been the comment so far above all of opponents with a Christian orientation, who include not only many theologians but also some (by no means all) lawyers and doctors. Men and women are not morally allowed to dispose of their lives, they all say. And doctors comment that the doctor is there to heal and reduce suffering, not to kill (the 'Hippocratic oath' is cited). They comment that more healthy and young people than old and sick people would call for mercy killing to be allowed: in the specific situation of hopeless illness this would happen only rarely. Lawyers add that particularly in the interest of a proper understanding of the freedom of the human person, the constitutional state cannot allow killing on request. And finally some theologians mention as a decisive argument that human life rests on a divine Yes to human beings. Life is God's creation and gift, and thus in principle is beyond human power to control.

It is evident that often such arguments, including those presented by doctors and lawyers, are anything but purely 'scientific'. They have an ideological colouring and an open or concealed philosophical or theological inspiration. Therefore the often hidden theological arguments in particular must be subjected to examination. Often doctors seem to be afraid of lawyers and lawyers afraid of judges; judges afraid of theologians, who threaten judges, lawyers and doctors with the wrath of God. So theologians should lead the way in clarification. What theological comment can be made on active help in dying?

The emergency

I openly concede that here I am not speaking impartially. This brings me back to my introductory comments on my lifelong reflection. It may help to show how important it is to discover the truth if here I insert a personal reminiscence which has become decisive for me. Almost exactly forty years ago, on 11 October 1954, I celebrated my first eucharist as a newly ordained priest of the Catholic Church in the crypt of St Peter's, Rome, with my family and friends. On the way there my brother, who was twenty-two at the time, had suffered a fainting fit. Nothing serious, we all thought; he was simply overtired and exhausted. After three weeks' convalescence in Italy he was taken to one of the world authorities on brain surgery of the time, to Professor Krähenbühl, in Zurich. The diagnosis was that he had an inoperable brain tumour between the cerebellum and the cortex. Periods in hospital with radiation and chemotherapy followed – but all in vain. Finally he was discharged as incurable. His condition grew worse and worse. One limb after another, one organ after another, ceased to function, a terribly slow process of dying with increasingly heavy pressure on the heart, circulation and breathing, lasting for weeks while all the time he was clearly conscious. Finally there were days of gasping until finally – almost a year to the day after the first attack – he choked on the rising fluid in his lungs.[30]

Since then I have kept asking myself whether this is the death that God gives, that God ordains. Must men and women 'submissively' accept this, too, till the end as 'God-given', 'divinely willed', even 'pleasing to God'? I still ask myself the question today, especially after in preparararion for a lecture on euthanasia,[31] at the invitation of Professor Ernst Grote, in the neurosurgical clinic of the University of Tübingen I was able to watch for the first time the opening of a brain, quite by chance a very similar case – and again the diagnosis was that it was inoperable, despite today's amazingly precise computertomography, laser techniques and microsurgery. 10,000 people in Germany fall ill each year with brain tumours, and a further 10,000 have metastases in the brain.

Of course I have been familiar with the traditional arguments of theology so to speak from my youth.[32] They go like this:

– Human life is a 'gift of the love of God'; it is God's 'gift', I am told, and therefore beyond our control. That is correct and remains true. But something else is also true: in accordance with God's will, life is at the same time also a human task and thus made our responsibility (and not that of others). It is an autonomy based on theonomy.

– It is added that human life is solely God's 'creation'. But in accordance with the will of the creator, is it not primarily a voluntary 'creation' by parents, and so from the beginning – a new experience of our time – something for which men and women are responsible?

– People must endure to their 'ordained end', it is argued in return. But my question is: What end is ordained? Does God really control the reduction of human life to purely biological life?

– 'Premature' giving back of life is said to be a human No to the divine Yes, a 'rejection of the rule of God and his loving providence'. It is tantamount to a 'violation of a divine law', an 'insult to the dignity of the human person', a 'crime against life', indeed an 'attack on the human race'. But (and truly I am not just thinking of my brother's case), what is the meaning of such lofty words in the face of a life which is definitively destroyed and in the face of intolerable suffering?

Behind these and similar arguments ('the argument from sovereignty') stands a misguided view of God based on biblical texts which are chosen one-sidedly and taken literally:[33] God as the creator who simply exercises sovereign control over human beings, his servants; their unconditional lord and owner, their absolute ruler, lawgiver, judge and basically also executioner. But not God as the father of the weak, the suffering, the lost, who gives life to human beings and cares for them like a mother, the God of the covenant who shows solidarity, who wants to have human beings, in his image, as free, responsible partners. So for the terminally ill our theological task is not a spiritualizing and mystification of suffering or even a pedagogical use of suffering ('purgatory on earth') but – in the footsteps of Jesus, who healed the sick – one of reducing and removing suffering as far as possible. For while suffering certainly teaches people to pray, in some cases it also teaches them to curse. There are said to be theologians who fear a 'society free of suffering' – and one asks what kind of world they live in. Indeed, there are theologians who in this connection call for a 'share in Christ's suffering' – as though Jesus would have argued for the intolerable suffering of a terminally ill patient kept alive on drugs.

However, in order to avoid misunderstandings, I immediately add: in opposition to certain advocates of active help in dying like the Australian moral philosopher Peter Singer, I am by no means of the opinion that people become 'non-persons' or 'no-longer persons' as a result of an incurable illness, the weakness of old age or definitive loss of consciousness.[34] One can understand how in particular those who are seriously ill react vigorously to such a view (and occasionally, in excess, even to any discussion). My standpoint is precisely the opposite: simply because human beings are human beings and remain so to the end, even when they are terminally ill (expecting death within a foreseeable period) or dying (expecting death in a short time), they have the right not only to a dignified life but also to a dignified dying and farewell, a right which may possibly (I say possibly) be refused them by endless dependence on apparatus or drugs. This can happen when in a process of dying which can last for hours or months, even years, only a vegetable existence is possible, safeguarded by all the techniques of pharmacological 'immobilization'. Therefore *a priori* the question cannot be dismissed: what is to be done in such cases?

Doctors, above all, answer that a clear distinction must be made between active and passive help in dying. I concede that conceptually that is certainly the case. But every doctor knows that in the increasingly rapid development of today's medicine the grey areas between active and passive help in dying are increasing considerably. To ask a specific question: why should the ending of a medical measure to sustain life – for example, switching off a ventilator – be only a passive help in dying and therefore one which is allowed? Moreover, many doctors feel that switching off a machine like a ventilator is quite an active measure. In terms of effect, which is quite clearly the onset of death, stopping a positive action (switching off a machine or disconnecting a drip) can be precisely the same as performing a positive action, say giving an overdose of morphine, and in some circumstances can even result in a much more painful death. It is often almost impossible to make a specific distinction in practice where a clear distinction must be made conceptually: the boundaries between all such terms as active and passive, natural and artificial, sustaining and ending life, are fluid. And the legal fiction, that passive help in dying is simply 'not doing something', seems to me to be a not very convincing *ad hoc* construction, if not a contradiction in terms.

So are we to condemn the numerous people

– who did not understand those American doctors who, supported by lawyers and courts, kept the unsaveable, unconscious Karen Ann Quinlan alive artificially for years and against the will of her parents;[35]

– but who, conversely, understood that Dutch woman doctor who put her semi-paralysed, depressive seventy-eight-year-old mother to sleep with an overdose of morphine and was therefore given only a token sentence;

– and also those who helped a woman author in Switzerland, hopelessly ill from cancer of the stomach, in accordance with quite definite rules of the Exit organization, to have the painless death which is allowed there?

In former centuries the issue was to protect against premature shortening of life (and this protection must also be guaranteed today against relatives greedy to inherit or irresponsible doctors or nurses). But in our time the issue is also increasingly the prevention of excessive prolongation of life which the patient thinks he or she can claim, which the relatives call for 'at any price' or the doctor forces on the dying (out of an interest in research or for ideological reasons). So what about active help in dying? Where some call this 'killing', others refer to 'compassion', 'mercy', 'grace', 'helping love'. What is the case? For a

Christian who is a disciple of the merciful Jesus, at any rate there must not be just an ethic of prohibitions and sanctions. What then? With discipleship of Jesus goes an ethic of the responsible shaping of life – from beginning to end.

Human responsibility even for the end

Today we no longer have just exceptional cases, as is shown by the figures from Holland, where at least there is more truthful information than there is in Germany.[36] Nor should it be said that here I am showing too much 'feeling' for those suffering in tragic situations and sacrificing hallowed principles. As a scholar and a theologian am I to switch off all feelings? The real question is what really are the sacred principles that are to be maintained in our day.

Anyone with a humane disposition is in favour of great respect for life and its unassailable dignity. The 'Declaration on a Global Ethic' approved by the Parliament of the World's Religions in Chicago in 1993 makes the following statement about the obligation to a culture of non-violence and reverence for all life: 'In the great ancient religious and ethical traditions of humankind we find the directive: *You shall not kill!* Or in positive terms: *Have respect for life*! Let us reflect anew on the consequences of this ancient directive: all people have a right to life, safety, and the free development of personality in so far as they do not injure the rights of others. No one has the right physically or psychically to torture, injure, much less kill, any other human being. And no people, no state, no race, nor religion has the right to hate, to discriminate against, to "cleanse", to exile, much less to liquidate a "foreign" minority which is different in behaviour or holds different beliefs.'[37] All this is to be given unqualified approval. But in Chicago the as yet unclarified special question of help in dying, about which there is as yet no consensus in any religion, far less between religions, was rightly bracketted off. On this point, first clarification and then consensus must be struggled for. Of course any human being hopes for an easy death, without bodily torment, oppressive anxiety and degradation. But what if things turn out differently?

Today even the more conservative theologians and bishops concede – at any rate, for example, by their modified position on birth control – that we are in a time of rapid change in our consciousness of values and norms, which is brought about not by the ill will of human beings but by the rapid changes in society, science, technology and also medicine. Not everything can come from the devil if today increasing direction of the processes of life is possible and is a matter of human responsibility. It makes me think when so many moral theologians who today still have problems with more active help in dying used to have similar difficulties with active, 'artificial' birth control, which they similarly interpreted and rejected as a 'no' to the sovereignty of God over life, until they were finally forced to recognize that God has made human beings responsible for the very beginning of human life – something, however, which the present Pope still does not recognize.

Would it not be consistent to assume that the same God now, more than before, had made the end of human life a human responsibility? This God does not want us to foist responsibility on him that we ourselves can and should bear. With freedom God has also given human beings the right to utter self-determination. Self-determination does not mean arbitrariness, but a conscientious decision. Self-determination also always includes responsibility for oneself, and this always has not only an individual but also a social component (respect for others). It would not be responsibility, but frivolity, arbitrariness, if for example a man in the prime of life, without a thought for wife and children, asked for help in dying because of a failure or a setback in his career. But would it also be arbitrary if a man who all his life has worked honestly and for others, yet at the end – after a clear medical diagnosis – is threatened by a tumour or perhaps years of senile dementia, total senility in old age, were to do the same thing, wanting to bid a conscious and dignified farewell to his family? In view of the question, 'In doubt does one decide for life or for the conscience?', must not respect for the conscience of the patient and his or her self-determination (even in the face of a possibly weakened freedom) have priority? Anything other than respect for conscience would seem to me to be an outdated medical paternalism. Conversely: no doctor can be obliged to undertake any medical practice against his or her conscience. But in cases of doubt doctors can be obliged to help in the search for another doctor.

Or is the patient perhaps to be comforted by doctors who are boasting of having given a woman almost one hundred years old a 'new hip' so that she can go home again and live for about another six months? Or by the fact that a severely burned woman, brought by rescue helicopter to a specialist clinic, could be kept alive another six months? To live another six months – is that good in itself? Have you ever seen an electrician who fell on to a high voltage cable (I have)? His head looked literally like a burnt cabbage (one could just recognize a displaced eye and a few teeth), and he was so seriously injured that he was unrecognizable and did not even dare to show himself to his family. Yet today he can still be kept alive indefinitely by the technical possibilities of medicine. It is not surprising that many people are afraid not only of pain and suffering but also of being imprisoned in a highly technological medical system, afraid of total dependence and loss of control over their own selves, drugged until they are dozy and sleepy, no longer thinking, no longer drinking, no longer experiencing anything.

There is no doubt about it: if someone afflicted by such a fate wants to keep his or her life, then such a person is to be respected and offered every help. Truly no one should be compelled or even urged to die a day or even an hour earlier than he or she wants. But conversely, no one should be forced to go on living at all costs. The right to continued life is not a duty to continue life; the right to life is not a compulsion to live.[38] So what if a person who is terminally ill finds life intolerable, and voluntarily, stubbornly and consistently expresses his or her desire to die? That there are cases like this should not constantly be denied: there are. One hears from doctors that so many completely disfigured people have been glad to have been kept alive. But there is hardly any talk of those who in their misery throw themselves from a high window in the clinic. There are so many fearful cases where one can understand it if someone says: 'My condition is intolerable. My greatest, last, wish is to die . . .' And how can anyone presume to decide whether another person shall live or die and seek to compel him or her to go on living and suffering? Certainly the human wish to die can only be the necessary condition for the doctor to intervene, and not the basis of the intervention. The basis can only be the well-being of the patient as he or she (and not the doctor or a third person) feels it.

One will hardly find an argument even in the Bible, which in any case knows no absolute inviolability of life, against suicide and voluntary death. In the Old Testament, the way in which Abimelech, Samson or Razis (in II Maccabees 14) kill themselves is reported in part with approval; the New Testament differs over the case of the traitor Judas. But nowhere in the Bible is suicide explicitly forbidden. Moreover Jesus of Nazareth nowhere described sickness as a fate imposed by God, to be accepted in submission; rather, he identified with sufferers in opposition to sickness, and in many cases provided help. And if even the first king of Israel, Saul, whose kingdom failed and who, when defeated by his enemies, finally fell on his own sword,[39] is not censured anywhere, could it be that other people who in the utmost distress have ended lives which they have no longer felt to have any human dignity will find a merciful judge? Who of us would want to judge whether a suicide in a state of neurotic depression or in a situation of extraordinary oppression is an 'impulsive reaction' or 'carefully thought out'? In the early Christian centuries those Christian women who preferred death by their own hand or with the help of others to brothels were explicitly praised by church fathers like Chrysostom, Eusebius and Jerome.[40]

There is no mistaking the fact that human responsibility has taken on another dimension in connection with the end of human life, as it has with its beginning, and men and women today are in a fundamentally new situation for which one cannot derive simple recipes from the Bible. But to what extent is this a fundamentally new situation?[41] For the first time in human history, in the past century human beings have succeeded, by improving living conditions and by extraordinary progress in medicine, in most cases in delaying death, which formerly did its work within a few hours, days or at most months. It has thus become possible to extend the time between the beginning and end of a fatal illness or total senility to many years. In this way human life, which hitherto embraced the phases of ante-natal existence, childhood, adolescence, adulthood and old age (and the majority of people never reached the last two phases), has been extended by a further phase: the years of terminal illness or senility. All this is the result, not of a 'natural' development to be attributed to 'nature' or the will of God, but of an almost Promethean effort on the part of human beings, who have themselves created this new phase. However, for some people it has become an almost intolerable burden. And in the face of this completely new situation, as earlier in the question of birth control, so also in help in dying, an ethic which attempts to be both scriptural and contemporary will consider its position and attempt also to find a responsible way for the last phase of human life.

A theologically responsible middle way

Of course I am also quite clear about the pernicious consequences that a deviation from the principle of the inviolability of human life can have. I know that as in the present unsatisfactory system, so too in a future system, there can be and will be abuses: for example, social pressure on patients finally to put an end to their lives and thus make room for younger people or bring relief to family and society. And I say equally clearly that a legal limit must be put on all macabre legacy-hunting by relatives and profit-orientated aids towards dying offered by health insurance schemes, and on the exploitation of transitory depressions. Such abuses must be fought against with every means, including the law, and also be made criminal offences.

The Reformed theologian Harry M. Kuitert of Amsterdam, who I find confirms my view in a number of respects, lays down the following conditions for granting active help in dying:[42]

1. The request must come from the sick person and not from relatives or nursing staff, and must be expressed in a well-considered and consistent way to the doctor in person (the expression of a constant desire for death?).

2. The suffering of the patient must justify such a request because it is intolerable or experienced as intolerable.

3. Help in dying is to be reserved solely for the doctor, who can help towards a gentle and not a botched or painful death.

4. The doctor has first to discuss with a colleague (an external colleague? – and also with the next of kin?) the seriousness of the request, the accuracy of the diagnosis of the patient's condition and the most responsible way of carrying out the measures which will end life.

5. Doctors have to make a note of their conditions (according to the new Dutch law the doctor must sent a report to the coroner, but normally there will be no prosecution).

It is primarily a matter for doctors and lawyers to work out concrete guidelines to remove the manifest legal uncertainty. The Netherlands has given an example of how this can be done. Clear legal guidelines for dealing with the problem of euthanasia could also remove the anxieties of so many people in Germany, and in other countries too, and help to avoid some conflicts of conscience among doctors. Why shouldn't the elementary principle that human beings have a right to self-determination even in dying be prescribed by the law? Or might a sphere outside the law be desirable specifically for this last stage of human life, in which, in a literal and highly personal way, an individual's 'To be or not to be?' is the question?

No, legal guidelines on areas of responsibility (with reference to killing on request, help in suicide and killing without the express wish of the person concerned) seem to me to be more consistent, both ethically and legally, and, in view of the large number of undisclosed cases, to be more truthful than recourse to an extremely vague 'emergency above the law' in which active help in dying will be 'tolerated' 'in individual cases'. In the latter situation patients are dependent on the autocratic decision of the doctor and open to possibly intolerable suffering at the very point when their helplessness is at its greatest. Dying cannot in any case be declared to be a free arena for medical diagnosis, as some doctors want and some legal judgments seem to presuppose. If the patient's 'head' is at stake (and not the doctor's), doctors cannot decide in a 'well-meaning' way 'over the patient's head', when their approach, while well-meaning, may possibly have been shaped by traditional thought–patterns and notions of faith on which there has not been sufficient critical reflection.[43] A clearly documented advance directive made by the patient is also a necessary part of the regulation, in the cause of legal clarity. This should be made – and here Switzerland is also an example – quite voluntarily and protected against abuse by numerous safeguards, but then it should be unconditionally respected by the doctor, provided that it does not go against the actual will of the patient.[44] This would spare doctors conflicts of conscience.

We should also reflect that an invocation of dangers is not in itself a refutation. After all my experience as a theologian's life on matters relating to the rejection of birth control, I am no longer impressed when people talk of breaching of the dam or going over the precipice. Indeed there are long-term general interests to be protected, but quite unmistakably there is also the oppressive distress of the dying of individuals. Certainly the 'living with cancer' that is recommended is possible for a while, but in some cases it can become completely intolerable. And here there should be an end to claims made particularly by theologians, but also by some doctors, that basically there are hardly any people who really want to die; that their wish to die is merely communicating in a 'disguised' way the desire for better care and human concern, so that 'a literal understanding of the request for euthanasia could only disappoint them'.[45] In any case, it is said, pharmacological medicine can do everything to ensure that the wish for termination does not arise at all.

But doesn't that make the doctor master of life and death and rob patients of autonomy where they want the decision of their consciences to be taken seriously? Of course there are temporary depressive moods and cases of loveless care and a lack of visits. But in return it can be asked: aren't also many doctors afraid of this last wish for active help in dying? So don't they sometimes withhold the necessary information and avoid a clarificatory person-to-person conversation? Of course not everyone who is willing to die will reveal this desire to a doctor or a pastor whose mind is closed, but in that case – as I have heard from more than one nurse – it will be expressed to the less prejudiced sister who does not forsake them in their dying days.

Certainly doctors have conflicts of conscience over the terminally ill. But I am not convinced by those doctors who – though there are also others – openly maintain traditional principles and even emphatically reject any active help in dying, but who, in many cases where palliative therapy has come up against its undeniable limits, *secretly* increase the dose of morphine more than is necessary.[46] There is no doubt that the well-being of the sick is the supreme law. But couldn't this supreme law itself require the sick person to be spared unending terror in favour of an end without terror?

Certainly, lawyers in particular see themselves confronted with conflicts of norms (between private law and public law) and have to worry about the effects of particular changes in the legal system as a whole. But I am not convinced by those lawyers who – though there are also others – without reflecting on their ideological presuppositions formally keep to the positive law (the *ius conditum*, without concern for the *ius condendum*), and who do not even recognize that particularly in the case of help in dying the 'highest law can result in the greatest injustice'.

To conclude: certainly theologians and churchmen in particular call for a special moral sensitivity. But I am not convinced by those – though there are also others – who in the case of help in dying, as formerly in the case of abortion, immovably advance rigoristic standpoints which are not understood even by the majority of their own confession. The churches generally, and the Catholic Church in particular, are called on to take a reasonable middle way between moral rigorism and moral libertinism in order to contribute to a consensus and not polarize and divide society by extreme positions; otherwise the German Conference of Bishops, like the Dutch Conference of Bishops, will ultimately (as in the debate over abortion) end up as the great loser, because, like the Dutch bishops, it has forfeited the support not only of public opinion, but also of the other Christian churches, indeed of most of its own church members.[47] Or perhaps we too will arrive at the point reached in France, where, according to the most recent opinion poll, eighty-three per cent of the population are guided in moral questions solely by their own consciences, and only one per cent (!) by the teaching of the church?[48]

Happily, even in Catholic moral theology today there is increasingly a move away from such rigoristic standpoints and an emphasis that the ultimate criterion must not be the maximal prolongation of life in the biological sense, but the realization of human values, to which biological life is subordinate. Thus as early as 1980 the Tübingen Catholic theologian Alfons Auer stated that the traditional theological basis for the view that human life is not under our control ('relationality to God') was 'ultimately unconvincing'.[49] So not 'every human suicide (and thus not active euthanasia either)' is '*a priori* absolutely and decisively to be rejected as immoral'. In his view the problem can be 'decided only by a responsible evaluation of benefits'. Indeed, according to Auer, every human being has 'a right for his or her conscientious decision to be respected by others. It is not within the competence of ethical reflection to evaluate personal moral decisions. It has the task of making visible what is binding in the various spheres of human life and expressing this incommunicable formulae.' And other theologians have expressed themselves even more clearly on this question, like the Protestant ethicists Joseph Fletcher and Harry Kuitert, and the Catholic theologians P. Sporken and A. Holderegger.[50] Karl Barth had already affirmed as an 'exceptional case' that 'not every act of self-destruction is as such suicide': 'Self-destruction does not have to be the taking of one's own life. Its meaning and contention might well be a definite if extreme form of the self-offering required of man.'[51]

So as a Christian and a theologian I feel encouraged, after a long 'consideration of the benefits', now to argue publicly for a middle way which is responsible in both theological and Christian terms: between an anti-religious libertinism without responsibility ('unlimited right to voluntary death') and a reactionary rigorism without compassion ('even the intolerable is to be borne in submission to God as given by God'). And I do this because as a Christian and a theologian I am convinced that the all-merciful God, who has given men and women freedom and responsibility for their lives, has also left to dying people the responsibility for making a conscientious decision about the manner and time of their deaths.[52] This is a responsibility which neither the state nor the church, neither a theologian nor a doctor, can take away.

This self-determination is not an act of arrogant defiance of God; just as the grace of God and human freedom are not exclusive, neither are God's predestination and human self-determination. In this sense, self-determination is demarcation over against others: just as no one may urge, necessitate or compel others to die, so too no one may compel them to continue to live. And is there a more personal decision than that of the terminally ill as to whether to end or not to end their suffering? If God makes the whole of life a human responsibility, then this responsibility also applies to the last phase of our lives, indeed, it applies even more to the real emergency of our lives, when it is a matter of dying. Why should this last phase of life in particular be exempted from responsibility?

How to die?

No false comfort, certainly not! But isn't there also an authentic, true comfort? There is not only a time to live but also a time to die, and there should not be a concern to delay this artificially or compulsively. 'For everything there is a season . . . a time to be born and a time to die,' says Koheleth, the preacher of transitoriness.[53] The truth in truthfulness — that is also my concern in this question. Here I do not want to proclaim anything from above in magisterial fashion, but merely to make my personal standpoint clear. I want to raise justified questions for reflection, which I hope will relax some of the tension in the great dispute that is already in the making, and prevent the fronts which are already developing from becoming rigid. Not least for that reason, at this point I am making a stand in the political discussion which has just started, so that this time, at least in Germany, in this question which is so serious we may avoid the party-political and church-political polarizations that made the question of abortion such a fanatical one. But that will work only if we can raise the debate to another level. To another level?

Yes, and that brings me back to the point which is decisive for me: precisely because I am convinced that death is not the end of everything, I am not so concerned about an endless prolongation of my life – certainly not under conditions which are no longer commensurate with human dignity. Precisely because I am convinced that another new life is intended for me, as a Christian I see myself given freedom by God to have a say in my dying, a say about the nature and time of my death – in so far as this is granted me. Certainly, the question of a dignified dying may not in any case be reduced to the question of active help in dying: but it may not be detached from that either. A dignified dying also includes responsibility for dying in keeping with human dignity – not out of mistrust and arrogance towards God but out of unshakeable trust in God, who is not a sadist, but the merciful God whose grace proves eternal.

Those who trust in God at the same time trust that death is not the end. In the light of the Eternal One, who alone can grant 'deep, deep eternity', the death of mortal life becomes transcendence into God's eternal life. As the old prayer for the dead in the eucharist has it, '*Vita mutatur, non tollitur*': life is transformed, not taken away. So should I be anxiously concerned how short or long this mortal life is finally to be?

Here on the basis of my faith I am not a jot more certain about my dying than other people: in the face of the majesty of death, self-confidence is least of all appropriate. None of us knows when and how our death will come about – and each individual dies his or her own death in an ultimate solitude. No one knows what will happen at the decisive moment, whether one will die in peace and tranqillity, or in panic, with anxiety, pain and crying. So I may not be certain of myself, but only of the forgiveness and grace of God in faith in Jesus Christ. But hope in this God should make my life different from a life without hope.

And it is to precisely that point that these comments have ultimately led: to a different, more serene, indeed more dignified, attitude to dying on the basis of a different attitude to God. Many men and women have gone this way before us. So if we have to break off all relations to human beings and things, then for believers, supported and helped by every medical art, and comforted (for those who wish it) by the sacraments of the church, this means a farewell to fellow men and women, an inward leave-taking, a return and homecoming to one's basic ground and origin, one's true home. It is a farewell which is perhaps not without pain and anguish, but which is said in composure and surrender, at any rate without weeping and wailing, and also without bitterness and despair. Rather, it is said in hopeful expectation, quiet certainty and (after all necessary affairs have been settled) embarrassed gratitude for all the good and not so good things that now finally and definitively – thank God – lie behind us.[54] Such a dying into God, with a sense of embarrassed gratitude, seems to me to be what we may hope for in trust: a truly dignified dying.

The Dignity and Indignity of Dying
as Illuminated by Literature
'If You Want Life, Prepare for Death'

Walter Jens

In order to have a reliable starting point for my reflections on dying, death and a dignified end, I shall begin by analysing a famous story, but one which only rarely, with the aid of imagination and alienating theatrical productions, is depicted in its – terrifying – realism. It is a section from the Gospel of Matthew, which is not meant to be read as a pious treatise but as the report of the beginning of a secular passion which could have taken place in Mauthausen, or equally well in Santiago de Chile, a Siberian gulag or a torture cell in Turkey.

'Then Pilate's soldiers took the man to the palace of the governor, where the barracks were, and gathered the whole battalion there, because they wanted to torture him. They stripped him of his clothes, put a red cloak on him, set a crown of thorns – made of thistles – on his head, put a reed in his right hand, knelt before him, and mocked him. "Hail, king of the Jews," they exclaimed with laughter. Then they spat at him, took the reed from his hand and hit him on the head with it, flogged him and finally took off the military cloak, gave him back his own clothes and led him away to the place of crucifixion.'

There is no doubt about it: if we did not know the name of the delinquent, we would read the text as a very precise, matter-of-fact description which is gripping precisely because it is so like a formal record. Here is the prelude to a death from which the executioners themselves seek to remove even the reflection, the last flicker, of human dignity.

The man who is tortured here, one among millions, stands as the representative of all the victims in the Roman circuses, clad in animal skins; of the witches dying a wretched death in the flames at the time of the Inquisition; and, not least, of course, of the victims of the twentieth century. He stands for the alleged enemies of the state, for children written off as subhuman, victims delivered to the gas chambers and the garrotte.

Jesus of Nazareth is a man who bears witness to the consequences of mocking human dignity, especially in the last hour. This man who was first flogged is an innocent victim. 'Flogged' is an innocent word, compared with the systematic 'technique' of scourging (as we have known since the days of Auschwitz, torturers work systematically with calculations). In Jerusalem they did not use ropes and sticks but scourges made of leather, into which long spikes and, like pearl necklaces, sharp pieces of bone and lumps of lead were inserted. And then there was the jacket of red cloth, the club in the fist and the straw garland on the head. 'He looks splendid,' the solders will have said, 'this king whom we have dressed in such finery.'

It was a fairground sport, then, that the torturers were mocking: the garland of laurel – woven out of thorns; the purple cloak – a filthy flag; the sceptre – a whip; the kneeling – mockery of 'number X', who faces extermination. Eight or ten or one hundred strokes, on the head, on the body, on the testicles: it didn't matter; Roman law did not recognize 'a maximum number of strokes'[1] . . . nor any control over the cynical mimes during the masquerades which were a prelude to death. The officers had some bright ideas. The exchange of insignia shows knowledge and intelligence: a crown of thorns instead of a diadem – no common soldier thinks of that; that needs study, instructors who know what they are doing when they parody the *proskynesis*, the worship due to kings – 'Hail, king of the Jews!' And to turn the kiss in honour of the ruler into an orgy of spitting: one soldier after another stood to attention, paid his respects, bowed the knee, and then got up, to spit straight in the face of the delinquent. If we accept the view especially of those scholars who have read the text most closely as a reliable document of literature, Jesus will not have stood but sat: 'Enthroned, the king receives the homage of his subjects'[2] – a king who has been made a buffoon: *ecce homo*. There he is, look at him, the laughing-stock!

Did Pilate want to evoke sympathy by presenting a tortured man? Was the flogging ultimately a means of saving the delinquent? Did the governor exploit the officers in the same way as they exploited the soldiers? The text, genuine testimony to that literature whose nature it is not to offer quick answers but to raise questions, provokes, line by line, the imagination of the readers. It compels the reader, reflecting on the archetype of an undignified dying, to look at what is described here, for a moment, from the perspective of the rulers, and there, beyond the stations of the cross, from the perspective of the victim. What did the delinquent feel – if he could still feel anything – at the moment when his arms were being bound to the cross-beam which he had to carry up to that post, high up on the hill, visible from afar, to which his body and the beam would be raised, before the assembled contingent would move to the last act, the nailing of his arms and feet?[3]

The more carefully we read the accounts of the passion, the more meaningful they become: because it is more basic, the process becomes vivid. No, this delinquent was not a pilgrim, who collapsed under the burden of the cross. The beam itself was too heavy for him, a beam which symbolically pointed to the end – the time when wood was added to wood, cross-beam to upright, with the block in the middle which served to hold the candidate for death as long as he was conscious. (Like the mockery, the crucifixion was also thought out at a desk. Minions do the work; those in charge calculate the relationship between physiological stamina and mental control.)

The Jew Jesus did not die but perished wretchedly, probably with a last tremendous, inarticulate cry. This was a cry, a prayer: 'I am mocked by my fellows and despised by the people' (thus the wording of Psalm 22). 'I am poured out like water, and all my bones are out of joint; my heart is like wax, it is melted within my breast; my strength is dried up like a potsherd, and my tongue cleaves to my jaw; you lay me in the dust of death. Yes, dogs are round about me; a company of evildoers encircles me; they have pierced my hands and feet. I can count all my bones; they stare and gloat over me . . . My God, my God, why have you forsaken me?'

Jesus' passion story denotes the last act of someone whose life was shaped by the interplay of hope and anxiety – an anxiety which drove the prophet of the Lord into solitude, which set him on the run in his lifetime and also made him require his witnesses to keep silent about his marvellous acts. 'See that no one learns of it. Do not reveal what I say to you. Let us depart before day breaks. When it grows dark again, I shall return.'

What shapes the accounts of an undignified dying is not defiance and heroic solemnity, nor a hero's death in glory, but that anxiety. This shape is given symbolic character in Luke's account of Gethsemane – again simple, and precisely for that reason depicted in a moving way: 'And being in an agony he prayed more earnestly; and his sweat became like great drops of blood falling down to the ground.'

So this was a wretched death; the pitiful end of a man who was tortured by anxiety more than anyone else. 'In all probability,' Eberhard Jüngel wrote in his book on death, 'Jesus died shrieking. We cannot rule out the possibility that he died in complete despair. We need to take this possibility seriously even if Jesus' violent death proved to be a consequence which followed from his preaching and his conduct, a consequence with which he himself had to reckon. At all events, we may not imagine the crucified Jesus as someone who died a heroic death. And in connection with the historical Jesus there can be no mention of the composure, indeed cheerfulness, with which Socrates died the death of a criminal.'[4]

A merciless death: Hector

So this was a wretched death, a dying which has always been a particular challenge to writers to describe (and the evangelists, too, wanted to be regarded as writers). How much this was the case is already evident from the first account of a death which takes place in the dust and not under heaven: Homer's description of the death of Hector, who is virtually abandoned both

by the Olympians and by the mortals, in Book XXII of the *Iliad*:
'Here at last the gods have summoned me deathward.'

Never before the Gospels has the death of a man, the
undignified and merciless death, been described so precisely and
carefully in the dialectic of cruelty and mercy as in the description
of the final battle before Troy: Hector's vain request for an
honourable burial at home; his vain appeal to the victor's mercy.
'I wish only that my spirit and fury' – what a reply to the request
to allow compassion and humanity to prevail! – 'would drive me
to hack your meat away and eat it raw for the things that you have
done to me. So there is no one who can hold the dogs off from
your head . . . but the dogs and the birds will have you all for their
feasting.'[5]

And then – a secret hint forward from Troy to Jerusalem – the
procession of soldiers who stab the flesh of the dead man ('See
now, Hector is much softer to handle than he was when he set the
ships ablaze with the burning firebrand') and who do not hesitate
to plunge their spears into the corpse – a prelude to the great
crescendo, the dragging of the dead body, the cry from all the
people and the lament of Andromache inside in the house. Again
there is a scene as a prelude. Here, before Troy, the *mater
dolorosa*, the mother of little Astyanax (in only a few weeks he
will be murdered); there the women under the cross – and in the
centre the inferno: the crying; the humiliation of the dead. Now
Achilles 'in both of his feet at the back made holes by the tendons
in the space between ankle and heel, and drew thongs of ox-hide
through them, and fastened them to the chariot so as to let the
head drag, and mounted the chariot, and lifted the glorious
armour inside it, then whipped the horses . . . A cloud of dust
arose where Hector was dragged.'[6]

Mindful of Hector and Jesus of Nazareth, the description of
their deaths by Homer and the evangelists, we could extend the
sphere of literature wider. Putting texts with different colouring
side by side, we would see such a scenario confirmed if after the
scenery of death we also compared the scenery of the dead from
the *Odyssey* and the Old Testament. How close in their
diminished humanity, as living dead, are Achilles and Samuel to
each other; how closely do Jewish and Greek princes resemble

one another in the quest of those others who, although shadows, keep their perquisites: the staff, the bloody helmet or, if one thinks of Saul, the priestly cloak, even after their death.

About 1800, in the dispute between Lessing, Schiller and Herder on the one hand and Novalis on the other, German literature conjured up an antithesis, the one side pointing to the discrepancy between death as the brother of sleep and the 'terrible' skeleton, and the other referring to the gulf between Greek libertinism and the way in which Christianity takes the last hour seriously.[7] This antithesis proves ahistorical if we reflect that the radiantly beautiful Achilles and Joseph, in the ranks of the dead, are to be thought of as brothers, and that the image of the skeleton, as the counterpart of death, who, as a brother of sleep, has put in the sickle, is a product of the late Middle Ages. The token of recognition for the early Christians is the fish: believers met one another in the sign of the anchor, and Jesus, akin to Hermes, was more a good shepherd and guide of souls than the judge of the world under the heavens.

And in particular this friendly collaboration which is at least hinted at shows that literature, whether of a Graeco-Roman or a Christian stamp, has certainly depicted glorious or sorry dying in war, in executions, in the exaltation of a martyr's death and the pathos of a last-minute conversion. Over the centuries it has presented the exorbitant – dying which moves heaven and hell, gods and human beings – in image and simile. But where is everyday death depicted, the dignified or wretched outbreathing of the soul after long sickness and great pain?

Everyday death: the ploughman's wife

Now at the beginning of the fifteenth century there is at least the complaint of the ploughman from Bohemia, who puts death on trial for taking away his dearest possession, his wife: 'I was her lover, she was my best beloved. You took her away, the delight of my eyes so full of joy. She is gone, my peaceful shield against adversity; she is gone . . . my bright star in heaven has gone, the sun of my salvation has gone to rest and she will never rise again – not she, not the shining morning star; her radiance has faded away. I have no more desires of the body; dark night is everywhere before my eyes. I do not suppose that there is anything that could restore to me real joy; for the proud banner of my joy has sunk into suffering.'[8]

Has the solitude of a widower, his anxiety and loneliness and emptiness, ever been described in a more moving way – the distress of someone who at the moment when he unreservedly acknowledges another as lover, spouse, bride and beloved, has to reflect that husband or wife will one day stand at the tomb, facing a return to an empty house in which clothes and writing equipment, sewing things and spectacles, everyday objects, evoke a no longer which will be felt even more painfully after long years of marriage than after short days of happiness? Here is the coat, and there, long out of date, is the vaccination card. Here an old bill, there a pen case, a book marked in pencil – that was important to him, that meant something to him – and now never again.

No, I shall never forget the moment when my friend Wolfgang Hildesheimer said to me after the death of his father: 'If my wife died before me, I could bear the ceremony, but looking at a brush which still had a trace of colour on it, the one bit of dirty red that she used for her last picture: that's unbearable.' (Now Wolfgang Hildesheimer died before his wife, and was spared solitude among the possessions of a woman who was no longer alive; the wish of husbands who have grown old, who are fond of referring to the life expectation of a younger wife – 'she will survive me, statistics guarantee that, moreover she is stronger than I am and will look after herself' – was fulfilled.)

A deviation – a short detour into the sadness of a widower's existence? An excursus for the sake of an excursus? Not at all. The reference to the 'ploughman's' complaint is meant to show that this dying, in which dignity and anguish meet – the non-violent departure from this life which those left behind must take, step by step – has been described in literature for centuries, at least after the event. It has been described from the perspective of the farmer as it was, two thousand years earlier, from the perspective of the lamenting Admetus for whom his wife Alcestis sacrificed herself in a pact with death in order that he might live. However, what happened beforehand at all events seems to be described in hints, with a view to the hour of the final farewell.

A gentle end: Alcestis

To demonstrate that, let us call to the witness stand Alcestis, as Euripides made her speak in the theatre of Dionysus through the words of a serving maid: 'She stripped the leaves from myrtle branches, not weeping, nor sighing, nor did the coming evil take the colour from her fair face. Then she hastened to the marriage bed in her chamber . . . and threw herself on the couch. Then, clinging to their mother's robe, the children wept aloud; she took them both in her arms, kissing them one after the other, as one who was about to die. And all the servants in the palace joined in the weeping, lamenting their mistress. To each she extended her hand for a last time.'[9]

A gentle end, restrained, kindly and full of human dignity, certainly: but compared with the great phantasmagoria of death in which the eccentricities of the description give it power to move the heart, the farewell scene in Euripides' *Alcestis* seems contained, cool and stereotyped.

Questions which the reader raises today are not touched on. What are the thoughts of a woman going to her death, whose husband has allowed her to sacrifice herself for him? How does she look at him when he is speaking and reading, worrying about the children and going to friends? What does she think when he comes home, loving but a little tipsy: grateful to have been able to forget for at least a few hours what Alcestis can never forget?

Furthermore, can one think of a greater anxiety about death than this? Will it happen today before the sun sets and the evening wind comes? Or tomorrow? In a year? Will the children already have grown up when it happens and death comes, somewhere at home, in company, at worship, during a short trip, a few days by the sea?

There is nothing of all this in the Greek drama; nor anything about the thoughts of Alcestis when she is saved, when Heracles brings her back from the realm of death, back to her children and her husband. How will she look on him ? In a friendly way? Or as a coward who was not bold enough to die himself but crouched behind the oven? Alcestis and Admetus – an old couple who no longer have anything to say to each other: a stubborn woman and an alcoholic?

Again, there is nothing of that in Euripides; nothing in his successors. But why? Perhaps because Alcestis is too heroic and Admetus too boring: he is no Orpheus who is ready to free his Eurydice from the underworld with his own strength (and a superb voice) instead of sending someone else into battle . . . but this Orpheus was also almost a god, sung until Gluck's Paris version of the *Orpheus and Eurydice* libretto by a castrato – a miraculous being like Farinelli or Caffarelli. The common view down to the middle of the eighteenth century was that people who go to the world of the dead have to have a voice which will span a full three octaves.

The approach: Ivan Ilyich

'Poor literature!' a first conclusion seems to be. It fails at the point where it is most urgently needed, as a kind of special help in life which has to give an example of a dignified or undignified dying, in its everyday character.

But this conclusion is premature. For at least a century we have been aware of what dying means for a person, having been instructed by prose (above all), drama and poetry. It took the slow approach to a form of sickness, cancer, to overcome on the one hand the stereotyped analyses of friendly dying, falling far short of the experiences of medicine (exceptions prove the rule), and on the other the apotheosis of an ailment, consumption, characterized with a highly poetical, romantic air, which figures as a kind of queen of nineteenth-century *belles lettres*. *La Traviata* departs, accompanied by the poor Hannele of Gerhart Hauptmann's *Hanneles Himmelfahrt*, or, still close to us, the brave Joachim Ziemssen who dies his 'Magic Mountain' death in Hofrat Behrens' sanatorium in Davos.

What the plague was once, after the fourteenth century, for the graphic arts (only after it do the skeletons and men with scythes appear in hordes on the stage), cancer becomes for literature:

dominating even where it is not mentioned, indeed where we remain uncertain whether the moribund person is dying from a carcinoma at all. The one decisive thing is that at the end of an era which was dominated by painless spiritualizing tuberculosis, an illness known for a long time, and already described in Hippocrates' time as 'stinking', comes into view, which, after it could be demonstrated even within the abdominal cavity by modern operative techniques in the time of the pioneering surgeon Theodor Billroth's time, provokes the literati like an avenging angel which has to be faced up to: in so many words or, by the mention of general symptoms, in periphrastic but verifiable talk.

I think that we can identify the precise moment when a writer for the first time ventured to approach death by literary means in a way which had previously been reserved for doctors – who, it may be mentioned in passing, wrote admirably. (Compared to the prose of Billroth and his contemporary, the pathologist Rudolf Virchow, the majority of contemporary novels are hacks' work.)

There was a man, just one man, Leo Tolstoy, who, always on the track of death, reflected on dignified and undignified dying, the wretched death of the rich and the end of the poor, steeped in humanity, the death of human beings and the death of trees. In the three short novels 'Master and Servant', 'Three Deaths' and his masterpiece 'The Death of Ivan Ilyich', he described, first, how a good life lived in accord with nature guarantees a serene end; secondly, how an arrogant human existence often governed by a counterfeit Christian faith leads to a miserable death; and thirdly, how so to speak everything that constitutes such a false existence can be revoked in the hours of death. In a snowstorm the landowner covers the servant with the warmth of his own body, gives him life, and in so doing also gives life to himself.

And then there is Ivan Ilyich, the protagonist of a story published in 1896, which for the first time no longer makes literature secondary, derived, subordinate to theology and medicine. Anyone who reflects on dignified and humiliating death, on dying that is self-determined and its dialectic (What can still be borne? What is beyond my powers?), cannot avoid first of all reflecting on the death of Ivan Ilyich. Here is the dying of a man which Tolstoy first of all considers from outside, from the perspective of the survivors, and then, with the help of a dramatic crescendo the end of which is almost intolerable, coming closer and closer to the dying person, turns into a constantly changing introspection: the slow approach as a poetic guideline.

To begin with, there is the chatter of the officials who consider the death of their colleague only in terms of who will be his successor, who will succeed the successor, who emerges as first, second, third, who has a chance and who does not. Then there is the irritated procession into the death room which jeopardizes the whist party in the evening (the motto of one of those who have come to pay their respects: 'nothing could interfere with the wrapping and cutting of a new pack of cards that very evening as the footman set out four fresh candles; in fact there was no reason to suppose that this incident could hinder their spending the evening as agreeably as any other evening').[10]

Tolstoy resolutely rejects a central demand of poetry and rhetoric that subject and style should correspond (death is not to be caricatured; a swineherd must not be elevated to the level of a king; the diction has to match the material, expressing the sad sadly, the modest modestly, the amusing wittily). He resolutely rejects this demand for literary congruence and stages a commiseration scene like a comedy: 'When they reached her drawing room, which was upholstered in pink cretonne and lighted by a dismal-looking lamp, they sat down at the table – she on a sofa and Piotr Ivanovich on a low pouffe with broken springs which yielded spasmodically under his weight. Praskovya Fiodorvna had been on the point of warning him to take another seat, but felt that such a remark would have been out of keeping with her situation . . . The whole room was full of knickknacks and furniture, and on her way to the sofa the widow caught the lace of her black fichu on the carved edge of the table. Piotr Ivanovich rose to detach it, and the pouffe, released from his weight, bobbed up and bumped him. The widow began detaching the lace herself, and Piotr Ivanovich sat down again, suppressing the mutinous springs of the pouffe under him. But the widow could not quite free herself and Piotr Ivanovich rose again, and again the pouffe rebelled and popped up with a positive snap. When this was all over she took out a clean cambric handkerchief and began to weep.'[11]

Can the comedy of farewell, in the sense of macabre contrariness, be described more precisely? Can it be surpassed in literature? Probably not, but in its grim interplay it can be repeated. When Thaddaeus Troll, tormented by depressions, put an end to his life, he insisted that in addition to a simple 'Our Father' a text should be read out which he, Dr Hans Bayer alias Thaddaeus Troll, had published a few years previously, at that time still playfully, under the title 'Words to be spoken over my coffin'. This document of literature was overtaken by reality when we, the congregation, gathered in Degerloch to hear Troll's testament. It went roughly like this: 'There you are, sitting in black suits which smell of mothballs and are too tight for you; for you've become heavier, all of you. And look! The pallbearers are already here, setting down the coffin with routine earnestness and taking off their hats. (And that really happened.). But you have only one thought, "If only I'd got saying something to the widow over with." (I confess, Thaddaeus Troll was right.)

In both cases there is a *danse macabre*, a dance of death which Tolstoy springs on us strikingly to distinguish the living and dying of Ivan Ilyich, after the event, by way of contrast, all the more meaningfully from the existence of a careerist whose only aim it is to observe conventions as scrupulously as possible by emphatically bringing out the difference between an examination of the files, a game and a supper. How different, by contrast, is the punishment of a solitary dying, introduced by a scene which, after Tolstoy, has taken on archetypal significance: a doctor examines a mortally ill patient, gives the diagnosis, and leaves his victim alone. Examples? Here they are. First Tolstoy: 'The doctor summed up as brilliantly as Ivan Ilyich himself had done in equally brilliant fashion a thousand times over in dealing with persons on trial . . . From the doctor's summing up Ivan Ilyich concluded that things looked bad, but that for the doctor, and most likely for everybody else, it was a matter of indifference, though for him it was bad.'[12]

Case studies in death: J. T. Malone, Philip Roth

A second example comes from another great account of dying, written seventy years after Ivan Illich, Carson McCullers' description of the last months of a pharmacist with leukaemia, called J. T. Malone. At the beginning of the novel, *Clock Without Hands*, Malone visits a friend, Dr Kenneth Hayden, who has his office above the pharmacy: 'The doctor did not look directly at him, so that his pale, familiar face seemed somehow eyeless . . . He sat silent at his desk and handled a paper knife, gazing intently as he passed it from hand to hand. The strange silence warned Malone and when he could stand it no longer he blurted: "The reports came in – am I all right?" The doctor avoided Malone's blue and anxious gaze, then uneasily his eyes passed to the open window and fixed there. "We have checked carefully and there seems to be something unusual in the blood chemistry." '[13]

A page or so later there follows, in Tolstoy fashion, but here quite openly, the quintessence: 'The long and short of it is, we have here a case of leukaemia.'

Finally, the third example, shaped by a fascinating variation. In Philip Roth's true story which appeared in 1991 under the title *Patrimony*, the narrator feels compelled to slip into the role of the doctor and tell the truth to his eighty-six-year-old father who has a brain tumour: side by side with a series of doctors, chosen to interpret the results of medicine to the dying man – at the same time truly and sparingly, precisely and very gently. 'Alone, when I felt like crying I cried, and I never felt more like it than when I removed from the envelope the series of pictures of his brain – and not because I could readily identify the tumour invading the brain but simply because it was his brain, my father's brain, what prompted him to think the blunt way he thought, speak the emphatic way he spoke, reason the emotional way he reasoned, decide the impulsive way he decided. This was . . . the thing that had ruled our fate back when he was all-powerful, and now it was being compressed and displaced and destroyed because of a "large mass predominantly located within the region of the right cerebellopontine and prepontine cisterns." . . . I didn't know where to find the cerebellopontine angles or prepontine cisterns, but reading in the radiologist's report that the carotid artery was encased in the tumour was, for me, as good as reading his death sentence . . . Maybe the impact wasn't quite what it would have been had I been holding that brain in the palm of my hands, but it was along those lines. God's will erupted out of a burning bush and, no less miraculously, Herman Roth's had issued forth all these years from this bulbous organ. I had seen my father's brain . . . a mystery scarcely short of divine, the brain.'[14]

There is no doubt that the 'cerebral exercises' of Philip Roth's description are infinitely far from Tolstoy's simple description of a dying man who feels the pains of death increasing in him, and becomes more and more aware of his solitude − of being lost among the living (apart from the only one who supports him in his struggle against death, Gerassim, the servant). At the end, after the last drop of hope has dried up in the sea of desperation, Ivan Ilyich falls into a deep black hole which suddenly opens up the second he recognizes that his wretched dying grows out of his miserable, spiteful, wasted life, a life which is his and no one else's. Now, suddenly, he knows that the moment of annihilation coincides with the moment of redemption: ' "So that's what it is!" he suddenly exclaimed aloud. "What joy!" '[15] There is no doubt, again, that in recent decades the literary description of dying has become increasingly precise, that its images have become more powerful, and that above all it has become more scientific; but there is no doubt that the decisive breakthrough already took place in those years when poetry finally lost its fear of analysing the last things, following the recognition that the decisive events in the sphere of human life take place in the brain and not − highly poetically, but in contradiction to physiology − in the heart. (One might think of Georg Heym's amazing pathological account of a dead body in 'Die Sektion'.)

In short, if for thousands of years poetry was a discipline which, in Kant's words, follows behind the truth that medical research brings to light instead of showing it the way, in the last century this has changed. However self-confidently Elisabeth Kübler-Ross may demonstrate with impressive pedantry the phases of death, literature − from Solzhenitsyn's *Cancer Ward* to Peter Handke's description of the suicide of his mother in

Wunschloses Unglück; indeed, from Tolstoy to Philip Roth – clarifies that unique quality of personal dying which even the most sensitive account of an illness can never describe. 'Death is always the same, but each man dies in his own way.'[16] That is how Carson McCullers' *Clock Without Hands* begins – and just how true the statement is is shown by the closing scenes of these three texts, written by Tolstoy, Carson McCullers and Philip Roth. They are significant for me above all because they bring out the private element by the alienating effect of poetry at the level of the authentic; but this is also shown by the accounts of dying, on the frontier between documentation and interpretation, which have been written by Anne Philipp or Simone de Beauvoir, confronted with the death of husband and mother. Finally, it is shown by those notes which dying men and women have made to help them to take stock of their lives in the last months. Here the personal is objectified by citing witnesses from the sphere of *belles lettres* (the key advocate is Montaigne), and by a constant discussion with the advocates of medical diagnostics and therapy.

One's own death: Peter Noll

I have to confess that for many years I never believed that an author could ever succeed in describing his own death so truthfully as to indicate a middle way between the Scylla of indecency, the surrender of the most intimate things which should not be disclosed, and the Charybdis of posing at a supposed distance. On this middle way the author's own experience, a resumé in the face of certain and very imminent death, is described in the form of a confession which gains its referential force on the frontier between confession and sober eye-witness testimony. No, I did not believe that a synthesis was possible until some years ago I read Peter Noll's 'Dictates on Dying and Death'.

A scholar and secret poet, a friend of my friends, a criminal lawyer and lover of theology, who wrote a treatise on 'Jesus and the Law', discovers after an examination that he has cancer of the bladder. The conversation with the doctor recapitulates literary patterns and in so doing testifies to its authenticity: the decision along the lines of Pavese, 'I will die and not let death get me', gains plausibility from page to page. Only not 'to get into the surgical, urological, radiological machine, because then I shall lose my freedom bit by bit. With ever-diminishing hopes, my will will be broken, and in the end I shall end up on the well-known death bed, around which all make a familiar circle. The antechamber to the cemetery.'

A man anxiously, with a rich vocabulary and also with serenity, at the end of his days, sketches out his funeral oration – in Switzerland a custom with an illustrious tradition. It is to be given in the Grossmünster in Zurich; he discusses with Max Frisch what should be said when the time comes, and disputes, in a very matter-of-fact way, but not suppressing secret hopes, with the prophets of the Old Testament. In short, he seeks out conversation partners, real, and even more imaginary, to learn from them what form a dignified dying takes, between this world and the world to come: 'I would like to speak with Socrates most of all, if I should meet him over there. He has all the properties that I admire: he was bold, shrewd, wise, tolerant – had no time only for stupidity if it was coupled with power. The brain' – and here is the key statement in the 'Dictates' – 'thinks God. That does not mean that God must exist, but it certainly means that the question of God cannot be dismissed and that empirical positivism is a lame duck. Pascal already saw that the infinitely small and the infinitely great, the microcosm and the macrocosm, provoke the question of God . . . Thought cannot think of anything without an origin. And the human brain is finally a creation from this origin. And this brain can think that there is the unthinkable.'[17]

In Peter Noll's 'Dictates' a man is writing in the face of death, which he confronts yet fears – simply because the last image which he offers his friends, like an actor who no longer has command of his text, is not his own but another's.

'Why may animals be put to sleep and not human beings?'[18] – a question that remains unanswered, like Bloch's 'Perhaps', which builds the bridge between the great nothingness and some last small 'oases of meaning' (a key phrase of Noll's, the most important) – unfortunately only a fragile connection.

Are there also oases of meaning in the beyond? Are they

conceivable? As zones in which that connection between God and meaning is preserved without which dying becomes absurdity? Question upon question, put by someone who in his last hours, writing in the world, attempts to keep very close to one of his secret partners and adversaries, Albert Camus – Camus, who identified writing with that poetic creation of 'conscious death', which is more than anything else capable of fighting against anxiety at death. However, as literature shows, this is a thesis which provokes contradiction: that comes in a letter of 6 August from the writer Maxie Wander, marked by cancer, dying, but still capable of the most precise formulations, to her friend Christa Wolf. It is published in her book *Living would be a Splendid Alternative. Diary Entries and Letters*, and runs: 'I've also wanted to tell you for a long time about the danger of getting it completely wrong. Can one write at any time and in any situation, and overcome the situation by writing? Isn't it some-times advisable simply to shut the desk, and perhaps even the books (?), in order to live in a different way, *simply to live*, to empty oneself or lie on the loor and listen, to oneself? Are we really orientated on one form of coping with conflict? . . . I don't entirely believe that you can only cope with these things by writing.'[19]

There is no doubt that had Peter Noll read these words, written three months before Maxie Wander's death, he would, while surprisingly agreeing with her over the question of coping with cancer, have firmly contradicted her. For him, like Kafka, writing was a form of prayer.

No trace of dignity?

And now, at the end of my reflections, immediately before things get serious and I cannot, any more than Hans Küng, hide in the shadow of the masters . . . now I imagine, after the men of letters and the theologians, the singers and the scientists, a doctor coming into the witness box. His name is Sherwin B. Nuland, and he teaches surgery and the history of medicine at Yale University. His book is *How We Die*, which became an international best-seller. Nuland is both a practitioner and a theoretician, a doctor and a journalist, with a brilliant knowledge of literature. He quotes Montaigne and literary treatises which are concerned with medicine, comparing them with the writings of his guild (mostly in favour of the literature).

In short, our last witness, Sherwin B.Nuland, may, without blushing, take his place among the writers: as a quite original example of the species which Robert Musil called 'Monsieur le Vivisecteur', endowed with a photographic memory and a strange preference for appearing invisibly (in social gatherings, instead of standing by the buffet, Nuland prefers the technique of secretly diagnosing party guests and their ailments). Whatever he does, he is a doctor, and everyone else is his patient – healthy, semi-sick, and deadly tired. He examines them, x-rays them and palpates them, probably in a dinner jacket: inventing mnemonics, making findings, outlining therapies.

Here, then, is a photograph: Sherwin B. Nuland, who, as a genuine writer, is at the same time an empiricist and an abstract artist. But he is also a man (and here he is particularly interesting to us) who throughout his book puts forward a quite definite thesis – a thesis which inescapably provokes a dispute with the men of letters whom I have introduced, and not only with them. According to Nuland, who attempts to take a middle way between 'poets, essayists, chroniclers, wags . . .' who 'write often about death but have rarely seen it', and 'physicians and nurses who see it often, yet rarely write about it',[20] and communicates skilfully, by the art of medicine and literature, that on the sickbed there is no 'dignified death'. What we call a 'dignified death' is in truth 'our society's universal yearning to achieve a graceful triumph over the stark and often repugnant finality of life's last sputterings',[21] but not a reality. It is the myth of a peaceful, mentally conscious end which has not the least in common with reality, in the course of which 'the disintegration of the dying person's humanity' takes place. His conclusion: 'I have not often seen much dignity in the process by which we die.'[22] Certainly, the survivors like to talk about it, but anyone who looks more closely – Nuland argues, referring to the testimony of a young man who supported to the end his friend dying of Aids – will note that dignity is unimportant for the dying and significant only for the survivors, who do not want to think ill of themselves (in the end they did everything they could in their efforts for human dignity in the shadow of death).

Nuland's second conclusion, now stated didactically and definitively, is: 'By and large, dying is a messy business. Though many people do become "unconscious and unconcerned" by lapsing or being put into a state of coma or semi-awareness; though some lucky others are indeed blessed with a remarkably peaceful and even conscious passage at the end of a difficult illness; though many thousands each year quite literally drop dead without more than a moment's discomfort; though victims of sudden trauma and death are sometimes granted the gift of release from terror-filled pain – conceding all of these eventualities – far, far fewer than one in five of those who die each day are the beneficiaries of such easy circumstances. And even for those who do achieve a measure of serenity during separation, the period of days or weeks preceding the decline of full awareness is frequently glutted with mental suffering and physical distress.'[23]

Anyone who speaks otherwise, Nuland insists, knows neither the misery of patients in the final stages of a decompensated heart defect nor the terrible finale to Aids. How can there be any dignity for someone subjected to intensive care which ultimately proves unsuccessful? There is no question of that. 'The patient dies alone among strangers: well-meaning, empathetic, determinedly committed to sustaining his life – but strangers nevertheless. There is no dignity here. By the time these medical Samaritans have ceased their strenuous struggles, the room is strewn with the debris of the lost campaign . . . In the centre of the devastation lies a corpse, and it has lost all interest for those who, moments earlier, were straining to be the deliverers of the man whose spirit occupied it.'[24]

How We Die: is this a book which gives no quarter? Its reception in America tells against such a label. The common view is that we should know what it means to die of a heart attack or cancer, a stroke, Aids or Alzheimer's disease, and that this knowledge is useful, especially in respect of the dying who, as Nuland portrays them lovingly, accept their death with great tenderness and humanity. Like Bob De Matteis, who celebrated

Christmas a last time with his friends and had put on his tombstone a sentence from Dickens, 'And it was always said of him that he knew how to keep Christmas well.'[25]

And then a last point, the decisive one. Nuland argues, cautiously, in a balanced way, castigating abuses, for active help in dying. He does so in passing, not following a general thesis. But line after line it becomes clear on which side he stands. Certainly not in the ranks of those who declare sickness, above all Aids, as the wages of sin, referring to God's wrath which fallen creation has to bear. Against this, Nuland argues: 'I prefer to believe that God has nothing to do with it [Aids is taken as representative of other suffering]. We are witnessing in our time one of those cataclysms of nature that have no meaning, no precedent, and . . . no useful metaphor. Many churchmen, too, agree that God plays no role in such things. In their *Euthanasie en Pastoraat . . .* the bishops of the Dutch Reformed Church have not hesitated to deal quite specifically with the age-old question of divine involvement in unexplained human suffering: "The natural order of things is not necessarily to be equated with the will of God." Their position is shared by a vast number of Christian and Jewish clergy of various denominations; any less forbearing stance is callous . . .'[26]

From this perspective Nuland supports Percy Bridgman, a Nobel Prize winner in physics, who continued his work until his last breath. When it was done and the cancer whose victim he was allowed no further study, he committed suicide. Bridgman regretted having to take the last step alone: 'I would like to take advantage of the situation in which I find myself to establish a general principle; namely, that when the ultimate end is as inevitable as it now appears to be, the individual has a right to ask his doctor to end it for him.' Nuland's commentary on this, written with reference to his colleague Timothy Quill, an internist who has given a most impressive analysis of support from the doctor in the hour of death based on mutual trust, is: 'If a single sentence were needed to epitomize the battle in which we are all now joined, you have just read it.'[27]

But what, we ask at the end of our meditation on dying, death and a dignified end, would Leo Tolstoy say to this sentence –

assuming that he lived in our time and was aware of the development of modern medicine? Could he bring himself to make the death cry of Ivan Ilyich, which lasted for three days, a *conditio sine qua non* of his knowledge in the last minute of life? We may be certain, I think, that Tolstoy in particular, the apostle of mercy, of compassion and of comprehensive sharing in the suffering of all suffering creation, would have agreed with Sherwin Nuland. So too would Carson McCullers, in respect of the death of the pharmacist Malone, which was peaceful and developed along the lines of a new simplicity and order: however, at what a price! Would Malone, as long as he still had the strength, in fact have surrendered everything that gave his existence humanity and dignity? Certainly not. On the contrary. He would have been ashamed of a man who capitulated, as G. T. Malone did in the hour of his death: 'What did it matter for him if the Supreme Court was integrating schools? Nothing mattered to him. If Martha had spread out all the Coca-Cola stocks on the foot of the bed and counted them, he wouldn't have lifted his head.'[28]

Death, as the poets make clear, going beyond Nuland and his combatants, can stand not only physically but also morally for the total revocation of the living.

And what about Philip Roth? He certainly is the key witness among the writers, for he did – but with how much torment! – what the advocates of help in dying would have required of him; he refused to allow his father to be attached to a respirator: 'He looked on that stretcher as though by then he'd been through a hundred rounds with Joe Louis. I thought about the misery that was sure to come, provided he could even be kept alive on a respirator. I saw it all, all, and yet I had to sit there for a very long time before I leaned as close to him as I could get and, with my lips to his sunken, ruined face, found it in me finally to whisper, "Dad, I'm going to have to let you go." He'd been unconscious for several hours and couldn't hear me, but shocked, amazed, and weeping, I repeated it to him again and then again, until I believed it myself.'[29]

Remembering Philip Roth's text, I think that if writers in future would join more emphatically than previously in the conversa-

tion between theologians, doctors and lawyers, they would have
something to say on the topic – the dead as well as the living.
Looking to Albert Camus, for example, who with his *alter ego*,
the protagonist of the novel *The Plague*, Dr Rieux, after the death
of a child (the cruellest death scene I know in literature) declares
the thesis of his counterpart, Father Paneloux, to be nonsensical,
namely that of course there are revolting things in the world, but
only because they pass our human understanding, and therefore
we should love what we cannot understand. 'No, Father, I've a
very different view of love. And until my dying day I shall refuse
to love a scheme of things in which children are put to torture.'[30]

In fact there is no lack of accomplices from the circle of the
literati (of both sexes) when it comes to correcting Nulan's theses
here (Is a dignified death really as rare as is claimed in *How We
Die?* Many doctors with whom I have spoken doubt this thesis),
to emphasize emphatically: no, a painful death can no more be
willed by God than a martyrdom somewhere in the world, or a
simple street accident, against which we protest with Kurt Marti:

> It did not please at all
> the lord our god
> that gustav e.lips
> died in a road accident
> . . .
> it did not please at all
> the lord our god
> that some of you thought
> such a thing happened to him
> in the name of the one who raised the dead
> in the name of the dead man who rose:
> we protest against the death of gustav e.lips.[31]

The right to die in peace and dignity

My conclusion is that literature, whose nature is to teach a kind of
art of living through simile and image, should, in the sense of
Freud's slogan, 'If you want life, prepare for death', take more
resolutely than before the side of those who, with the Swiss

doctor Urs Peter Haemmerli.[32] time and again draw our attention especially to that fifth right of the sick and dying, the right
not to have to suffer but to be able to die in peace and dignity: as
the Universal Commission of Human Rights of the Council of
Europe has formulated it in article 2.

Literature should show, vividly and precisely, how people
today have died, wretchedly and in an undignified way, because
over their beds, invisibly but with discernible contours, hangs the
picture of Adolf Hitler, whose actions were implemented against
'subhuman life', under the treacherous guise of euthanasia, year
after year create millions of new victims because we do not reflect
enough that murder is one thing and self-determination another.
It cannot be said often enough that the attack on life which is
allegedly subhuman has nothing to do with a dignified dying that
is not imposed from outside but is desired by individuals, real
human beings: it is the opposite to that.

From this perspective, it should be a task of literature (of course
this cannot be an order, but writers should reflect more resolutely
than before), to ask whether Ulrich Bräker, the author of the
book *The Life and Natural Adventure of the Poor Man in
Tockenburg*, was not correct when he regarded merciful death as
a human right and in March 1797 noted in his diary: 'Has . . . the
all-gracious creator of all things commanded nature to torture
this person and that slowly to death?' Certainly it is the calling of
the doctor 'to comfort suffering humanity, to come to the help of
destroyed nature . . . But if he finds it impossible to remedy the ill
and exposes his patient to years of suffering, may he not make the
same ripe for death somewhat sooner, help him to rest and in this
way come to the help of languishing nature? Or is it his duty to
make the slow step of nature even slower, slowly to torture such
an unfortunate to death over years? I do not believe so – at any
rate, were I a doctor, I would not make the latter my duty.'[33]

Thus Ulrich Bräker, in 1797, in a purely theoretical argument.
He does not claim that his view is binding on anyone but thinks
the question of a dignified dying through to the end for himself –
'I certainly do not want to decide, but I can think what I will' –
and at the end of his meditation asks the doctor to show a last
service to the incurable and, as a merciful Samaritan, to release

him – of course, we may add, going beyond Bräker, only if the incurable person gives good and reliable reasons for wanting this.

Millions of people, like Hans Küng and me, could go about our work with easier minds if we knew that one day a doctor would be at our side: not a specialist, but a family doctor like Max Schur, one of the most admirable men of this century, who did not hesitate to give his patient Sigmund Freud the fatal dose of morphine. However, he did this only after Freud had borne many operations with unprecedented courage and with full awareness of the torments he was taking upon himself. On 21 September 1939 Freud reminded his physician and friend of the pact which they had made at the moment when the cancer which was destroying the dividing wall between the oral and the nasal cavities became manifest for the first time. 'Dear Schur, you will remember our first conversation. At that time you promised not to leave me in the lurch when the time came. Now there is only torment and no more sense.'[34]

If only we knew that for everyone there were physicians, women like Gertrude Postma or men like Timothy Quill or Max Schur – physicians who without their white coats speak in the evening with people and not with patients, involve them in their plans, listen to a friendly 'Be honest, what would you do in my position?', and finally bring in the family doctor who, after a long knowledge of the dying person, testifies to what is tolerable for the person today and tomorrow, for the person and the family, in whose memory the dying person wants to remain as a subject claiming autonomy and not as an undignified caricature of a being whose wretched image blots out all others! It would certainly be easier to live with the knowledge, 'You too have a Gertrude Postma who mercifully relieved her mother of intolerable suffering; you too can make a pact with someone as courageous and humane as Max Schur.'

Yes, it would certainly be easier to live with this knowledge. The childhood belief, deeply rooted in the unconscious, that each of us is immortal, is losing its power;[35] by contrast, the notion that it is part of human dignity to be finite and to be able to die would, in combination with the statement 'everyone has the right not to suffer', become the maxim of a society which again gives the human being the dignity of a *regula omnium viventium*, to use the terminology of a doctor, Petrus Hispanus. He was not only an admirable man of letters, pious and with a philosophical training, but also, in 1276, when John XXI became Pope, calmly combined theology and literature in a 'Preparation for Life' imposed on both disciplines.[36]

What does Kurt Marti, the man of God and songwriter from Bern, a common friend of Hans Küng and of mine, write – note, in the subjunctive!

wish
that all share
prayer of the prayerless:
that one day death will come to us
suddenly and gently
from one second to another

softly nimbly
like gems in the rock
like fish in the sea
life would leave us
if only we knew
this wish granted us[37]

Discussion

Dignified Dying from a Doctor's Perspective

Dietrich Niethammer

The discussion on dignified dying sparked off by the contributions of Hans Küng and Walter Jens is important and necessary. However, some people may be surprised that a paediatrician has been asked to speak as a representative of the medical profession since, as is obvious, paediatricians are responsible for the beginning and not the end of life. I would like to begin with a personal experience.

Dignified dying

It is precisely thirty years ago since I was faced for the first time with a child dying of cancer. I was a student at the time. Jutta was a twelve-year-old girl with tumours all over her body. She was already so weak that she could no longer stand. Her body had become a skeleton and she refused all food. Only her big dark eyes still seemed alive, and she turned them to me as I came in, only to look past me immediately into space when I tried to say something to her. Jutta no longer spoke to anyone, either the doctors or the sisters, or even her parents when they came to visit her twice a week and desperately tried to spread some cheerfulness. For all of us, Room 3 was intolerable. We only went in when we had to, and then left it again almost in flight. Our words often stuck in our throats. One day Jutta died, and no one was with her. I was both relieved and ashamed at the same time. Jutta was brought from the ward at dead of night and we never said anything about her again. It was as if she had never existed.

Later, as a young doctor, I watched many people die, like Jutta, without saying a word, alone, abandoned, often in a tiled bathroom or in a storeroom, since there were no single wards.

And time and again, sitting on the bathtub or on an upturned bucket and waiting for the last breath, I saw Jutta's big eyes in front of me, as when just once she had looked at me for a little longer, while I desperately tried to engage her in conversation.

Since Jutta's undignified death, much has changed. We broke the tabu which had been handed down to us and began to talk to patients: about their illnesses, about the possibility of dying, about dying itself and life after death. Both young and old people were equally preoccupied with these questions and we could make some promises to them: they would not die alone and they would not have terrible pain, since modern medicine has invented not only machines but also methods of treating pain which work very well and need not have the side-effect of making the patient drowsy. And we have long learned that we are not telling patients anything new when we tell them the 'truth'; we no longer know more, since we are just confirming what they already know. And so the terrible speechlessness has largely disappeared.

Walter Jens has spoken of Peter Noll,[1] who planned his funeral and discussed with Max Frisch what was to be said 'when it gets to that point'. Children and young people plan their funerals, look for presents for friends and relatives, want to see certain people, and think about the future of their parents, brothers and sisters. Like Noll, they face up to death, which they fear as much as he did. Recently a fifteen-year-old boy asked to be buried where his mother lived, and not where he had lived for years with his father. At least in death he wanted to be near to his mother again. It helps if one talks about one's concerns. The dying want to continue to control their lives as much as possible, and much of what they do aims at being as certain as possible that they will not be forgotten when they are dead.

And frequently children and young people determine the point when they no longer want to come to the clinic and when they cannot take any more. Karl, a seventeen-year-old boy, suffered from a return of a tumour which was resistant to therapy. He had hardly any complaints, but needed regular blood transfusions. From time to time he looked worse, but usually he was cheerful and relaxed. One day he asked me, 'What would happen if I stopped having blood?' I explained to him that he would then get increasingly tired, and one day would go to sleep and not wake up. For a while he said nothing and reflected. Then he said quietly: 'In that case, I want to stop having blood now. Could you please also get my parents? It's so difficult for them, but I can't take any more.' Then I sat on his bed for a while without speaking. Karl's parents accepted his decision, which he could make because he had confidence in us and in them.

Four basic questions

I now want to ask four questions which are urgently prompted by the two previous contributions:

    1. Is anxiety about medicine justified?
    2. If that is the case, then what is the reason?
    3. Is killing on request an adequate solution to the problem?
    4. Should advance directives be a binding testament?

1. Are anxieties about the dominance of apparatus in modern medicine or the fears of getting into a process in which one loses one's freedom step by step (thus Noll) justified? Or the anxiety about a type of medicine in which, according to Hans Küng, 'one person presumes to decide on the survival or death of another, wanting to compel them to go on living and suffering'? Yes, I certainly believe that these anxieties are justified. Far too often it is simpler to go on with treatment than to think about ending it, and too often courses of treatment are begun when a conversation about stopping them would be more sensible. Therapy to control pain is still often useless, and far too often patients are abandoned by doctors before they die. The Zurich theologian Robert Leuenberger once said: 'The inhuman treatment of a dying person in truth does not begin with the artificial prolongation of his or her life, nor is a dying person given the fatal push by being refused the administration of important substances. Both things happen when intimate companionship is withdrawn from the sick person – perhaps months before he or she dies.'[2] And that is precisely what many doctors do, perhaps because they believe that they are responsible only for survival. An ancient physician's

oath runs: 'The task of the doctor is sometimes to heal, often to relieve and always to comfort.' That is equally true today, but modern medicine often wrongly seems to put the emphases differently.

2. So if fears are justified, is this simply the fault of medicine? No, medicine is part of society, and what does society do for those of its members who are dying and fatally ill? In many hospitals the availability of single wards has hardly improved since Jutta's death thirty years ago. Yet despite this, aren't many dying people sent to hospitals by members of their family? And how often are these members of the family present at death? Who is really holding back the lawyers who – increasingly in Germany, as in the USA – are pressing the doctors towards ever new action and justification? Aren't many people demanding the right to maximal therapy as the right to health? So it is not just medicine which leaves people alone when they are dying; it is also the members of our modern society, who often do not want to have anything to do with the dying.

3. So if it is the failings of medicine and society which cause the dying to be left in isolation, is the only solution active help in dying, which is then regulated by law but cannot prevent abuse in individual cases? I think that the question must first be raised whether medicine and society are not called on to reflect on their attitudes. The appeal for death to bring release is often a cry for closeness and companionship and a request not to be left alone. Nuland[3] is quite right when he emphasizes that only in a small proportion of cases does dying take an acceptable course for the person concerned. In my experience there is never anything idyllic about dying. It is bound up with pain, being alone, anxiety, anger, helplessness, resignation, denial and despair. It is not so important in what sequence these come about.[4] Nor can much of this be prevented, since it begins much earlier than the moment which all fear. It is often terrible when someone has to go through all this alone. But despair often alternates with hope, and knowledge of death and hope for eternal life exist side by side. It is this juxtaposition which also often makes it so difficult for us

survivors to support the dying. Finally, dying is also a farewell, which is as important for those who are departing as for those who remain behind. What I have said should make it clear that, for many reasons, the dying need dialogue with those who want to support them.

Often doctors are unsure and do not want to make a mistake. But if members of the family do not abandon a patient, then, like Philip Roth,[5] they can stop the doctors if they intend nonsensical treatment. Without Philip Roth's presence, his father would have been on a ventilator to the end, as the law prescribes. But this did not happen, because Roth felt responsible for his father.

Children and young people constantly make clear to us that they want to talk about their anxiety and what oppresses them. Obviously for many of them this makes it easier to bear. And what is often done in the case of adults? Frequently the situation is made clear to a partner, who is advised not to talk about it to the patient, who in turn is given no information. The result is an end to dialogue between partners. So the patient dies alone; he or she is abandoned although someone is there. That, I think, is undignified and unworthy.

Of course there are people who suffer beyond bearing. Precisely at that point they must be supported by doctors, who must not be afraid, say, of administering too high a dose of morphine as the only way of ending their suffering. A sixteen-year-old girl, who suffered desperately from lack of breath because of a lung infection, asked me to put her in an incubator and ventilate her. I had told her that this was the only possibility of relieving her of the terrible lack of breath, but that she would probably not wake up again and die. 'Then do it!', she asked, and died next day in narcosis. Being forsaken by everyone, including the doctor, is the most undignified way of dying. But death on request is no alternative to this.

There remains question 4. Is an advance directive – made under certain conditions controlled by law – binding on doctors? The desire for such a directive often comes from young people, frequently under the impact of specific events. The tragedy of the individual case is generalized. Here, however, the motive force is the desire not to experience what one has seen (or more often, only heard or read about) in another instance. This desire is never typical of the point in time when its fulfilment can be asked for. The experience of doctors is that such a desire arises very rarely, even if it is a possibility for patients. How can a directive be binding if mental functions have been irreparably damaged by injury or disease to the brain and therefore a repudiation or a confirmation is impossible? Advance directives can at best help us to get closer to patients whom we do not know well.

Healing – relieving – comforting

To sum up: the anxieties are justified, and there are indeed failings, but the solution is not legal regulation for active help in dying which attaches great importance to the advance directive. The solution – which is certainly necessary – must be sought at quite a different level.

Walter Jens said that he and Hans Küng could go on living better if they knew that they had a friend among doctors like Sigmund Freud's friend, who ended his suffering after many operations which he bore bravely. This appeal to us doctors cannot be ignored. But the decisive thing for Freud was the friend who stood by him to the end and did not leave him alone. However, one cannot sue for a friend or regulate friendship by law. And I think that the request for help must be a matter between doctor and patient which is the concern of no one else, whether court or assessor. Perhaps that is utopian, but experience shows that it is the way. 'Friends don't leave one another in the lurch,' a twelve-year-old boy once said to me. 'Friends don't lie,' he added, because he noticed my hesitation in asking when he would die. That is what children and young people expect from us, and can expect from us.

So after all I have said, my view is that we do not need any legal control. Our present possibilities are enough, if doctors and others in our society take seriously their obligations towards fellow men and women. If that happens, no old person need fear that the doctor will be convinced by members of the family that it is better for him or her to die than to live. And how have people come to expect us doctors to be ready to put a patient to sleep if the patient wants this or once wanted it? The argument that only a doctor can do this does not hold water. Any drug addict knows how to give an injection. The price for the freedom of the individual is a fearful burden on a profession the prime task of which is the preservation of life. Even having to switch off a ventilator when it no longer makes sense to keep it on often causes us much thought. Are others really clear what they are asking of us in making active help in dying part of our task? The only legal regulation which we doctors should ask for is indemnification against legal action if we have supported our patients adequately.

Sometimes heal, often relieve, always comfort! If we take this seriously, then I am certain that very few people will ask for fatal injections. And where there is no other way, relief and comfort may not be refused. Mercy and love of neighbour are certainly the substance of the medical profession, but they are also an essential part of interpersonal relationships. So the members of a society cannot just ask this of the doctors — though they may expect it of them — but should also examine their own behaviour. To let someone die with dignity is a task to which we are all called. Here it is clear that today and in the future doctors will have to see this as one of their main tasks. Then anxiety about medical apparatus will also recede; the apparatus will be given the status it really deserves, and human dominance will no longer be endangered. In an article on 'Humane Dying', Paul Sporken says that it is pointless asking who should give personal support to the dying.[6] This would basically be determined by sick persons themselves, by indicating from whom they wanted to receive help. This could be the doctor, the nurse, a relative or also a pastor. That is precisely what we find in everyday experience. According to the Bonn theologian Franz Böckle, 'Dying is a part of living. Death and dying do not coincide. Dying is the way that human beings have to take in the last phase of their lives before death. It is always a longer or shorter piece of life. The support that we give the dying is therefore also help in life, help in the last difficult part of our life.'

Jutta's lonely life was undignified. An injection could have ended her suffering earlier, but even this would not have spared her her solitude and the undignified dying in which that resulted.

The Possibilities and Limits of Help in Dying: A Lawyer's View

Albin Eser

I am somewhat uneasy about commenting on this topic as a lawyer. For is not dying such an intimate process that it must seem alienating for the law to play a part in directing it? Nevertheless, the law must also attempt to protect this sphere; for at any rate dying represents the end of life, and to this degree the state – to some degree as a 'guarantor' of life – must see that human life continues to be protected.

The role of criminal law in the boundary area between living and dying

A protection against premature shortening of life

This is the first aspect of protection we need to discuss. As a law aimed at preventing abuse, criminal law is a 'mistrustful' law. It may not simply have in view worried relatives and the well-intentioned doctor, but must also take into account their heirs who think that their entry into their inheritance should be hastened, or the nurse for whom care of the incurably ill person has become an apparently senseless burden, or even the doctor who may perhaps, conversely, think it necessary to keep a patient alive in order to be able to test the effectiveness of the therapy. Whereas in focussing on the interest of patients to determine their own futures it may be argued that society should not forcibly bar the way to someone who wants to leave this world, the legal system must ensure that people do not *fall* out of this world or are even *pushed* out of it who, if their true will were heeded more attentively, would really prove not to want to leave it. In other words, criminal law must prevent permission for suicide from becoming an excuse for social neglect, and help in dying from becoming pressure towards dying. To this degree, criminal law is aimed at protection, a protection which traditionally has stood in the foreground, namely protection of the patient from a *premature shortening* of life.

Protection against inappropriate lengthening of life

However, contrary to this traditional view, we need to reflect that recently concern for patients has in some cases been governed by an interest which is the opposite. For death can not only be manipulated by a premature shortening of life, but also be postponed by extending life beyond its so-called 'natural end' by the use of modern techniques of reanimation. This possibility is not unlimited, but it can be realized to such a significant degree that from the perspective of society the question arises whether and to what extent the individual should be able to claim the use of such measures to prolong life or to what degree such an extension of living and dying should also be forced on the individual against his or her will. This poses two completely new tasks for criminal law.

First, it has to clarify the degree to which the doctor should be able to evade the *excessive claim* of a patient for a *prolongation* of life. Here, however, it is already questionable whether doctors should simply be able to do this on the basis of their own assessment of the treatment, or only in connection with certain criteria, or taking into account the competing interests of other patients.

Conversely, however, it is also necessary to reflect on the interest of the patient against an *imposed prolongation* of life, for example by a doctor who believes it permissible or even necessary to postpone death at any price. If I have understood correctly the pioneering book by Paul Moor, *The Freedom for Death* (1973), this above all was the direction in which he believed men and women should be protected. That there is a need for protection here can hardly be denied: from a doctor who may be dominated by a particular research interest, but also from a doctor for whom the personal well-being of the sick person generally threatens to be suppressed by a principle of success, the primary aim of which is the efficiency of medical treatment or the gaining of new objective knowledge.

The most important basic principles and cases

What does this mean for the possibilities and limits of help in dying? This question is not easy to answer, since apart from paragraph 216 of the Criminal Code, which provides for a mitigation of punishment in cases of 'killing on request', in German law there is no provision, let alone a conclusive legal ruling, which is explicitly concerned with help in dying. Therefore it is necessary to resort to general principles.

The prohibition against killing another person

First, mention should be made of the fundamental prohibition against killing another person. To this degree a strict tabu is imposed: the other person should have no permission to kill. There are only three important exceptions here: in self-defence, in killing in war, and in some countries also the death penalty.

Suicide exempt

What is apparently incompatible with the prohibition against killing is that a person can commit suicide with impunity, provided, of course, that the action is a voluntary and responsible one.

'Killing on request' a criminal offence

These two principles of the prohibition against killing another person on the one hand and the freedom to commit suicide on the other necessarily come into conflict only when a person intent on dying wants to make use of the help of another person to leave this life. Should this third person be as innocent of this offence as the one who is weary of life? Or should the prohibition against killing another person also apply in such cases? German law – and this is a third basic principle – has decided for a middle way by providing for a reduced sentence (from six months to fifteen years, as compared with the normal sentence for murder) for a person who, to quote the wording of paragraph 216 of the Criminal Code, 'has been governed by the explicit and serious desire of the dead person'. This expresses two things. First, that in the case of such a 'killing by request' both the injustice and the guilt are obviously less serious than in other forms of killing. Secondly, by not letting even the perpetrator motivated by compassion get off with complete impunity, the fundamental impregnability of the prohibition against killing another person remains. However, this should not apply to:

Merely taking part in a suicide no crime

Since, as I have already pointed out, suicide as such is not a punishable offence, in Germany – in contrast to, say, Austria and Switzerland – abetting and help in suicide is not in principle an offence. That means that in the case of active help in dying the decisive question is whether this is to be understood as 'killing by request', which is an offence, or merely as 'help towards suicide', which can be offered with impunity. How this difficult and certainly also not unproblematical line can be drawn in individual cases has already posed many puzzles to jurisprudence and legislation, and even now it cannot be said to have been completely clarified. But at any rate the predominant view at present can be summed up like this: as long as the final decision over the bringing on of death remains with the person concerned, help towards this is to be regarded as non-criminal assistance in suicide. But as soon as the decision over the onset of death decisively lies in the hands of a third party, there is a case of criminal killing by request – though in every case it has to be presupposed that this is a well-considered, free decision of the person concerned, free from obstacles to insight and judgment.

However, uncertainty has been introduced into this reasonably clear distinction by the fact that in some circumstances the possibility of a criminal action arising out of an omission to fulfil obligations has to be taken into account. This happens in two ways. First, in the case of a suicide which is to be regarded as an 'accident', according to paragraph 323 of the Criminal Code, anyone who does not provide the possible help that might be expected in order to save the person committing suicide can be charged with 'failure to offer help'. Secondly, a 'guarantor' responsible for protecting the person concerned, a category which according to paragraph 13 of the Criminal Code may include relatives and even the doctor giving treatment, can be guilty of killing by neglect. This is beyond dispute in a case where someone with a duty to help allowed a person committing suicide to die, when that person *a priori* did not have a free and responsible will to die or a change of mind could be recognized. By contrast, to the degree that the will to die can be regarded as matter of free responsibility, the question arises whether by respecting this will, the duty to help and thus the criminal offence of letting someone die is not a factor. That brings up a further group of problems.

Complicity in allowing a person to die

Although our legal order does not regard the consent or even the desire of the person being killed as any justification, and thus does not regard this act as legitimate, the right of the patient to self-determination is nevertheless not completely without significance. Certainly this is a block to active killing. But the right to self-determination has so far been respected, at any rate when through it the patient is said to be able to have an influence on the process of dying by, for example, prohibiting further treatment in order to be able to die in peace. To this extent, from a legal perspective the principle holds that it is not so much the well-being of the patient as primarily the patient's will that is the supreme principle.

However, this principle has also been shaken to some degree by the legal pronouncements of the Federal Court of Justice. The Federal Court, too, attaches very great importance to the right of the patient to self-determination, particularly within the doctor-patient relationship. Therefore it is also to be seen as an expression of the basic right of a person to retain physical integrity where – as the Court put it earlier – he (or she) 'refuses to surrender his bodily integrity even if in so doing he will be freed from a life-threatening complaint'. By contrast, according to decisions of the Federal Court, the will to die is not to be respected in principle. That was also confirmed in the case of Dr Wittig in 1984. Nevertheless, here too the Federal Court decided on an acquittal, allowing the doctor to exercise his own judgment on his own responsibility as a framework within which the right of the patient to self-determination could be taken account of. At any rate this has recently been reinforced by the recognition of the Federal Court in the Kemptner case that if the presumed wishes of the patient could be established reliably, treatment might be terminated even before the final process of dying began (judgment of 13 September 1994).

One-sided termination of treatment

In contrast to the group of cases mention above, in which the patient explicitly asked for treatment either not to be started or to be stopped, here we have a very much more difficult group of cases of one-sidedly allowing patients to die. These are cases in which the patient is completely incapable of making a decision or at least cannot be spoken to, perhaps as the result of arriving in hospital unconscious as the victim of an accident, so that it is impossible to discuss with him or her in a rational and human way whether the treatment should be stopped. It might be psychologically too much to confront the patient with this question, or because of age or sickness the intelligence of the patient might have already declined to such a degree that it was no longer possible to discuss this question with him or her. Is the doctor to have any obligation here to do all that is necessary before the beginning of brain death – which in the present view is the point at which human beings cease in the legal sense to be 'human', and the point at which the safeguards against violating the body and protecting life come to an end? Until a few years ago that was still the view of the Munich criminal law theorist Paul Bockelmann (now deceased). By contrast, the quite dominant view today is that it must be possible to break off treatment even before the onset of brain death, even if it is impossible to consult the patient about this. However, there is a dispute as to whether this is generally to be done on the basis of a diagnosis from the doctor, or whether the law must not have an interest in the doctor, too, being obligated to particular criteria. That is certainly the case, above all because the patient has to know on being admitted to a hospital that everything will be done up to a certain point – in other words how much will be done for individual patients is not just a matter for the personal assessment of the doctor. Moreover, of course doctors themselves have an interest in such certainty and clarity, because in the end this is the only basis on which the necessary trust can flourish. The problem is simply what criteria are relevant here.

If one looks through the medical literature on the question, the main point made is whether further measures to preserve life still make any 'sense': thus the criterion of meaningfulness is to be decisive. But surely this question of meaningfulness could be a highly subjective one? Could not the toleration of pain which to one person seems quite meaningless still be an act of moral testing for someone else? To allow the doctor to intervene here as a kind of guardian by leaving it to his wisdom whether prolongation of life is still meaningful or already meaningless stands in suspicious contradiction to the self-determination of human beings, including the dying, which elsewhere is thought of so highly.

So others attempt to depart from this very vague and subjective criterion of meaning, the 'meaning of life', and put the emphasis on whether the death of the patient is 'fated' and inevitably predestined. But here, too, by contrast, must we not ask whether it is not the primal task of medicine to keep hindering natural fate by artificial means? For would not medicine give itself up if it failed to keep intervening artificially in the process of dying?

Instead of this, yet others attempt to differentiate between 'ordinary measures' to prolong life, which doctors in any case feel it a duty to take, and extraordinary measures which are to be used at the doctor's discretion – a distinction which had already been made by Pope Pius at the famous anaesthetists' congress in 1957 and which was then applied above all in the United States in the

Quinlan case (1975). But must we not ask whether these distinctions are not too dependent on the particular state of medicine, indeed perhaps even on the possibly retrograde customs and institutions of the individual hospital, to lead to a reliable criterion of distinction?

Reflection on the purpose of the doctor's task

In my view, we can avoid all these difficulties only if we reflect on the real purpose of the doctor's task. But that will not be possible without also acknowledging certain basic anthropological principles; for at the latest when asked about its purpose, medicine, however technological, must understand itself as more than an applied natural science. It is there to help people to create the physical and psychological presuppositions for their personal fulfilment and to preserve these as long as possible. And this question of the purpose of the doctor's task has already been given very different answers in the course of history. Sometimes this task has been extended and sometimes it has been reduced again. It seems to me that today, too, we face a revolution over this question. Certainly the task of doctors is still circumscribed, in that in addition to the duty to heal and to relieve pain, it also includes the duty to preserve and prolong life, so that for example in 1955 such an important physician and politician of culture as Willy Hellpach could postulate that doctors are 'unconditionally preservers of life, or they cease to be doctors'. By contrast, however, the Council of Europe feels unable to see the prolongation of life as 'an exclusive purpose of medical practice'. This seems to me to be a very important statement. Though there may be different nuances, for a long time the Council of Europe has not been alone in this view; for in turning from a more scientific and technological way of thinking focussed on success, medicine is rightly beginning once again to reflect on its primarily humane task of serving the common good of men and women rather than seeing its essential aim as technical competence or the isolated preservation and restoration of individual organs. Its lofty but at the same time more limited goal is not quantitative biological prolongation of life for its own sake but the possibility of at least a minimum of ongoing fulfilment. If this goal proves no longer to be attainable, further medical efforts are fundamentally no longer in the service of the patient. And in that case they can no longer be required by the law.

If we attempt to draw conclusions from this for criminal law, on the one hand we need to maintain the duty to preserve life. But on the other hand this irrevocable obligation to preserve life may end where on the basis of irreparable loss of any capacity of reaction human beings are robbed of the possibility of further perception of themselves and further fulfilment; and that is the case at the latest when there is demonstrably irreversible loss of consciousness.

The 1977 Swiss guidelines for help in dying seem to me also to end up with a similar regulation in stating that the doctor may cease treatment if the patient can no longer lead 'any conscious life related to the environment with the formation of his or her own personality'. However, we should reflect whether this formula is not too vague. For must not the law have an interest in establishing in some way by some specific medical criterion the point in time from which conscious life related to the world around is no longer possible? That could be irreversible loss of consciousness. So that would be the one decisive point and it would be legitimate to break off treatment from the moment when on a human prognosis the patent could never regain consciousness.

Preserving human dignity

A further aspect follows from the principle of human dignity. However, here I do not want to be misunderstood: I am in no way one of those people who think that simply to attach a person to an apparatus is to violate his or her dignity, since that would mean that we would have to take the whole of modern medicine back into the last century. Rather, in my view human dignity is violated only when the issue is no longer one of keeping a person alive and the individual has really become just the object of other interests – like purely medical skills – or where the delaying of the onset of death is conditioned solely by financial interests (for example, of the relatives, because they need a grandparent to live into the next fiscal period, or – evidently by no means an insignificant factor in the United States – the hospital has an interest in keeping its patients as long as possible). In such cases the issue is no longer that of the patient as a person. The patient is no longer being served; rather, by keeping the patient alive quite other, alien, interests are. If in this way the patient were degraded and became a mere object, the doctor would have not only the right but even the duty to break off treatment; therefore doctors in such an instance may oppose even the contrary views of relatives.

A disproportionate expense?

Finally in this area we need to consider yet another aspect, though we need not argue for it unconditionally: the disproportion between aim and expense, in other words the question whether and to what degree material interests may play a role in breaking off treatment. Certainly it may be shocking at first sight that life is related to the expense associated with it; for if on traditional principles life cannot be calculated against life, how much less can life be calculated against other material goods? However, it seems that on this point, too, legal principles have already been overtaken by the reality of the modern hospital business: what already begins with the need for doctors to use their limited possibilities selectively, and is continued by the impossibility of paying for therapies which might possibly be important for life, quite often ends in the question whether the use of intrinsically possible measures to prolong life are in fact still worthwhile.

'Technical termination of treatment'

In the discussion of terminating treatment so far, the primary focus has been on the case of terminating therapies. But similar principles must in fact also be applied to so-called technical termination of treatment – when an apparatus is switched off or a patient is taken from a so-called 'life island', a measure which can bring about or at least accelerate his or her death. Certainly lawyers argue whether this can be seen as an action, in which case it would be forbidden, or is merely leaving someone to die, in which case it would not be a criminal offence, according to the same principles as in the 'medicative' termination of treatment discussed above. At all events, by far the most dominant view is that the issue is the social significance of such termination. Just as the doctor is (only) omitting to do something in stopping an attempt at resuscitation which began with massage, so too the doctor is only omitting to do something when interrupting the work of a machine at a higher, more technological level.

Active killing

With that I want to leave this area, to consider some perspectives on active euthanasia. That this problem, too, has not been removed was already made clear in the canton of Zurich in 1977 when as the result of a referendum the legislature was asked to investigate whether active euthanasia should be allowed in a certain sphere. The current demands of the (private) German Association for Humane Dying are also moving in a similar direction. And not least the most recent regulations in the Netherlands – though these are more procedural – have been a further stumulus to a widespread refusal to prosecute active and passive help in dying. As far as the current German law is concerned, in essentials the following cases need to be differentiated.

Relieving suffering with a risk of shortening life

In cases of active killing, first of all the situation in which the doctor is primarily concerned with relieving pain and takes into account some risk of causing death is comparatively unproblematical. Certainly even these cases of so-called *indirect euthanasia* are relatively difficult to cover in law because if the doctor is aware of the risk that a dose of morphine may hasten death, in law he is acting with the so-called 'conditional proviso'. Therefore according to a view which prevailed for a long time even this was forbidden. However, today the quite prevalent view is that where the doctor is acting with the prime aim of relieving pain and thus does not intend the risk of death but only takes it into account, and this happens with the actual or presumed agreement of the patient, the doctor is then justified (though there is dispute as to whether one calls this a justifying emergency or – as I believe – it must be treated as a 'permissible risk').

Deliberate killing

The cases in which death is not only taken into account as a risk but is deliberately aimed at as a means of removing pain, as in that of the Dutch doctor Gertrude Postma van Bouven, where the aim was deliberately and consciously to cause death (1971), are in quite a different category. It must be said quite clearly and firmly that such *direct euthanasia* is not allowed under German law; in other words, here paragraph 216 of the Criminal Code would intervene with a minimum sentence of six months imprisonment. Of course that applies even more in cases in which the question is not the relief of pain but – as for example in the Nazi euthanasia actions – the so-called 'extermination of those unfit to live'. Rightly, our constitution simply does not allow such discrimination based on the value of life.

The pros and cons of a legalization of direct active euthanasia

It is clear that the law as it now stands can bring doctors into conflict with their own convictions: this happens above all where the patient wants to die, and would perhaps also kill himself or herself, but perhaps is unable to do so (as, for example in cases of paralysis), and also where simply letting a patient die does not seem adequate, because in some circumstances it would be torture to deprive the patient of everything that he or she still needs. Should not the doctor in some way – and perhaps similarly also the relatives – be given the possibility here of acceding in an emergency to an explicit request for death?

Arguments for active euthanasia

At first sight the harshness of the present law seems to tell in favour of a new regulation and thus for a degree of legitimation for active euthanasia. In favour of this, it can also be argued that the distinctions which we now have in our law somehow do not appear convincing because they seem arbitrary.

That can already be demonstrated by means of the distinction between help in suicide on the one hand (which is not a criminal offence) and killing by request on the other (which is). If a doctor leaves an overdose of sleeping tablets on the bedside table to make it possible for a patient to commit suicide, he is commiting no criminal offence, but merely giving help in committing suicide. But if the same overdose is injected by the doctor, then under paragraph 216 of the Criminal Code he has to expect a minimum sentence of at least six months; and even if we may suppose that such a sentence would be appealed against, this is not much comfort for the doctor. Here there is an urgent question whether the ethical status of these two modes of action is really so different as to justify such different consequences.

Moreover the distinction between relief of pain with the risk of death (which is legitimate) and deliberate killing as a means of relieving pain (which is not) can easily lead doctors into hypocrisy. Here doctors need only think no more about the risk that an injection might prove fatal, or at best convey the hope of a good outcome, and they can already justify the legitimate risk.

Similarly, the different treatment of passive and active help in dying does not seem completely free of arbitrariness. May the question whether a ventilator may really be switched off with impunity depend finally on whether this has to be understood dogmatically as a mere failure to act or as a positive action? In that case would an injection which had a rapid effect in principle and in every case be ethically and legally more reprehensible than the removal of a drip which lengthened the torment of dying?

The negative social and psychological consequences of a regulation about help in dying which is felt to be too harsh are no less weighty; for if under the pressure of public opinion, say, in Holland sentences end up as no longer than a week, such a discrepancy between the will of the law and the sentence in fact discredits the law.

However, the demand to allow euthanasia would be based on a weak foundation if it were possible only to cite inadequacies in the existing law in its favour. Far more significant is a positive demand: the right to die with dignity. If we reflect on more than a thousand years of the calumniation of suicide and then only its gradual acceptance as an act of desperation in human weakness, we can see that the demand for a 'right to one's own death' amounts to what I would call an almost Copernican shift in attitudes to life. Dying, too, is understood as a part of the fulfilment of personality and thus of life. Here the insight that the important thing about life is not only its quantity, namely its temporal dimension and duration, but also its quality, namely the possibilities for what seem to a person to be meaningful development, come into play. In the light of such considerations, we are almost forced to raise the question whether making euthanasia on request possible should not take account of this interest in the patient's self-determination and self-fulfilment.

Objections to the legalization of active euthanasia

However, some objections to such demands cannot be over-looked either. I shall begin with the central point: the right to death. It is already problematical whether there is such a right; many of our constitutional lawyers think that our Basic Law, which accords a right *to* life (article 2), does not necessarily accord a right *over* life. Now of course that need not exclude the possibility that one can argue that the state should respect the right to suicide. But such a 'freedom to die' does not as yet provide a basis for killing on request. For we must be clear that where there is a concern to declare killing on request legitimate, the right to die is being turned into a *right to be killed*. Anyone who does this overlooks the fact that a right to be killed must necessarily also involve another person in the killing, and that strictly speaking the recognition of such a claim would have to be matched by the duty of the state to make someone available for this killing. So it is not surprising that for example in Sweden the question has already been discussed whether, if active euthanasia on request is allowed, the state must not also make available institutions in which this demand can be met. One can hardly be offended that doctors would resist such a role. So at all events, what is left is a middle way, namely that the state refrains from punishing those who want to help someone weary of life to achieve freedom to die by their active participation.

It is understandable, moreover, that the limiting criteria which have been discussed – like the intolerable level of pain, the imminence of death, etc. – are of course open to all kinds of abuse and that doctors are afraid of saying that a person has only a week, a month or a year to live. This heightens the problem of all these solutions. But in my view the most difficult thing is to demonstrate that a person really wants to be killed. Might not the expression of such a wish be a last cry of hope that the inevitable could still be averted? Particularly in the case of those who are seriously ill, must not one posit a marked ambivalence between hope and resignation? Is a free decision possible when someone is in pain? How can outside pressure be averted? It is thought that such distortions can be avoided by giving permission at least thirty days before the decisive action, with the signing of a document in the presence of witnesses. Others even want to involve a committee. But however much this concern for certainty is to be welcomed, we must ask whether it does not introduce an atmosphere into the death room which tends to turn 'death with dignity' and dying as the last realization of one's own selfhood into its opposite.

In addition to all these practical problems, we should also reflect on important socio-political consequences, for example the possible effect of bursting the dam if certain exceptions to the tabu on killing are allowed. Certainly we should not suggest that the legitimation of voluntary euthanasia is at the same time the first step towards involuntary euthanasia. Nevertheless, we should at least be made to think by the fact that in some books – for example Ruth Russell's *Freedom to Die* (1975) and Marvin Kohl's *Beneficent Euthanasia* (1975) – the case for involuntary euthanasia has already been argued, but disguised with trivializing constructions of what is voluntary. For example, when Russell argues that it should be legitimate to kill mentally damaged children or senile men and women, how can one speak in such cases of a 'voluntary' decision to die? Or if 'non-involuntary euthanasia' is identified with 'voluntary euthanasia' – which is accepted anyway – and this awkward expression is then simplified as 'voluntary euthanasia', the word-play disguises the real human problem. A 'beneficent' death – for whom? For the persons concerned? Or essentially only for those around? What seems most decisive to me is that euthanasia infringes and thus weakens the principle of the inviolability of life; for by being subject to control, life would at the same time lose its inviolability. Once this tabu is broken, why should it not be possible to control life in other cases? Why only when a person gives up on himself or herself? Why not also when they are so irrational as not to do so? In that case, what claim would those who are no use to society or those who had become a burden have to be carried by relatives or by society? What argument would the hopelessly sick have against the expectation of those around them that they would ultimately make use of their right to be killed? Could not this freedom to die ultimately turn into a lack of freedom to live?

Finally, one cannot dismiss the suspicion that permission for euthanasia could easily become an excuse for more deep-seated social neglect. If we reflect that never in its history has medicine made such tremendous progress in the sphere of relieving pain as in our time, then it seems paradoxical that today in particular the call for the legitimation of euthanasia is resounding so loudly. One of the explanations could be that on the one hand people are getting older and older, and on the other that they are losing their functions in society very much earlier. Thus physiological death has already long been preceded by 'social death'. And as a result, continuing life has apparently lost all meaning. People simply wait for their end, often already outside society, impersonally, in old peoples' homes or hospitals. It seems understandable that people attempt to counter this literal 'dying out' in solitude by again making death personal – if only by having a say about the time when it comes. But is this what they really want? Is this not perhaps a desperate reaction to escape the neglect in which they are abandoned by a society that is not particularly well disposed to old age? And doesn't society make it too easy for itself if it further consolidates these neglects by making euthanasia permissible?

That should not be taken to mean that I want to rule out all attempts also to take account of the motive of compassion. However, there are problems about the course that should be adopted. So I found it very impressive that at the 1975 Bielefeld symposium on 'Suicide and Euthanasia as a Problem for the Humanities and Social Sciences', at which scholars from very different disciplines, from both Germany and abroad, had gathered, it was the quite specially committed defenders of active euthanasia, like Gerhard Simson of Sweden, who at the end of the day had to concede that the state could probably never declare active killing legitimate if it were not to suspend its duty to protect life. But – and this is certainly worth serious discussion – that does not exclude the possibility that the law should nevertheless take account of the motive of compassion. One of the possibilities might be that while the verdict of guilty should be upheld, in such cases there should be no sentence. I think that this would take account of both interests. On the one hand the state could express the fact that one can never declare active killing of life that has been born to be legitimate, and that therefore a verdict of guilty is inevitable. But on the other hand it could be conceded that the pressure of motivation, for example on a doctor who is acceding to a request, can be so strong that for subjective reasons the action should not carry a penalty.

A new draft law on help in dying

Much of what has been discussed and proposed earlier is now of course on an uncertain legal foundation. Therefore some years ago a 'Working Party of Professors of Criminal Law and Medicine' undertook in an 'Alternative Draft of a Law on Suicide' (Stuttgart 1986) to bring legal clarification to those forms of help in dying which today can largely be regarded as acceptable. As I myself made a substantial contribution to this draft and hope that the reason for it is self-evident, I shall content myself here with a few brief indications of its aims and main ideas:
– Creating legal clarity for all concerned;

– An attempt at the most comprehensive regulation possible which is understandable in its own terms;

– The safeguarding of life without any compulsion;

– The view that life is worth protecting and the rejection of any differentiation in its 'value';

– Making possible the optimum relief of suffering;

– Self-determination of the person concerned as the basis of the regulation;

– Priority of help *in* dying over help *to* die;

– Respect for responsible suicide by limiting the obligation to save contrary to the patient's wishes;

– In cases of doubt over responsibility, priority for the preservation of life: *in dubio pro vita;*

– Retention of the principle that killing on request is a criminal offence, but in exceptional cases without the imposition of a sentence;

– Objectifiable criteria for medical diagnoses;

– No explicit criminalization of a refusal to accede to the desire of a patient to die.

In this sense the alternative draft law on help in dying proposes that paragraph 16 of the Criminal Code on 'Crimes against Life' should be supplemented as follows:

§214 Termination or omission of measures to preserve life

(1) Anyone who terminates or omits to take measures to preserve life is not acting against the law, if

1. the person concerned explicitly and earnestly requests this or

2. the person concerned in medical opinion has irrevocably lost consciousness or in the case of a severely handicapped neonate will never gain it or

3. the person concerned in medical opinion is otherwise incapable of making a declaration about the acceptance or continuation of treatment and on reasonable grounds may be assumed to have been opposed to this treatment given the duration and course of hopeless suffering and especially imminent death or

4. in the case of imminent death given the suffering of the person concerned and the hopelessness of any curative treatment the

application or continuing measures to preserve life is in medical opinion no longer appropriate.

(2) Section 1 also applies to cases in which the condition of the person concerned arises from an attempted suicide.

§214a Measures to relieve pain

Anyone who as a doctor or with a doctor's authorization takes measures in the case of a terminally ill patient with the patient's explicit or presumed agreement to relieve serious conditions of suffering which cannot otherwise be removed is not acting against the law even if the onset of death is hastened as an unavoidable consequence.

§215 Failure to prevent a suicide

(1) Anyone who neglects to prevent the suicide of another is not acting against the law if the suicide is the result of a voluntary decision stated explicitly or of what can be recognized in the circumstances as a serious decision.

(2) Such a decision cannot be presumed especially if the other person is not yet eighteen years old or if a free expression of will is hindered as under sections 20 and 21 of the Criminal Code.

§216 Killing on request

(1) If anyone has been led by the explicit and serious request of the dead person to the killing then a sentence of between six months and five years imprisonment is to be imposed (unchanged).

(2) On the presuppositions of section 1 the court can remit the punishment if the killing serves to end a serious state of suffering which the person concerned can no longer bear which cannot be removed or relieved by other measures.

(3) Such an attempt is a criminal offence (previously section 2).

These proposals already gained remarkably great approval at the 56th Conference of German Lawyers in Berlin in 1986, the criminal section of which was discussing 'A Right to One's Own

Death?' Certainly – apart from recommending 'dispensing with punishment' in the case of killing on request (216 section 2 of the Criminal Code), it was impossible to resolve on any further steps in legislation. But this was not, say, because the proposals of the alternative draft would have been unacceptable, but because these proposals already corresponded to the dominant view and were to form the basis for legal practice. From this perspective at any rate the alternative draft can be understood in substance as a manifestation of existing law.

I should not end without emphasizing quite specifically as a lawyer that criminal law can really be only a last emergency brake for avoiding possible abuses. So it would be necessary first of all to clarify the social and political background in order to do justice to modern needs in an appropriate way. That means that more needs to be done not only in hospitals but also within families concerned to ensure that those who are marked by death can experience their dying as still part of their realization of themselves. Perhaps in this way 'manipulated' death might even resolve itself – as a basically unfree pseudo-liberation of the person concerned.

An Open Discussion

Hans Küng, Walter Jens, Dietrich Niethammer, Albin Eser

Hans Küng: Colleagues, ladies and gentlemen, I am sure that there is no one here who has not been deeply impressed by the two contributions to the discussion which we have just heard. I am first grateful above all to my Tübingen colleague Dietrich Niethammer for having spoken so personally. Walter Jens and I are already aware of his deep sense of responsibility and his open attitude; this was also why we asked him to take part in this discussion. We also presumed that he would not be completely in agreement with us. But you will certainly have noticed that we may not be so far apart as seems at first sight.

Of course everything that Herr Niethammer has said about dying children spoke to me from the heart. I was also deeply moved by his accounts of conversations with sick people, and that of course applies to young and old alike. Finally, his critical comments on medicine also moved me. This ideal of the Children's Clinic in Tübingen is far removed from what one can hear about dying in clinics elsewhere.

I would also like to say one other thing straight away. I much appreciated the fact, Herr Niethammer, that you did not make the usual moral insinuations which keep cropping up in talk about any dignified dying that deviates from the norm, insinuations that one is falling in with the spirit of the age or being carried along by the prevailing mood. I hope that what both Walter Jens and I said has made it clear that our attitude is not the result of a sudden idea and a single conversation, but that such thoughts have preoccupied us for years. Therefore Walter Jens and I claim that our moral attitude is as high as all those who put forward a more conservative view. I have expressed my personal conviction as a theologian, arguing from a different image of God, from the example of Jesus and belief in eternal life, and in this way am seeking to adopt a different attitude to dying. These are my real arguments, and I am glad that you have tacitly recognized them and have not said, as so often happens, that this is simply giving way to the spirit of the age. That is not our concern.

No, our concern is to find an ethically responsible way in the question of dying. I think that the four of us here on the podium, the doctor, the lawyer, the literary critic and the theologian, first of all share a common front to the degree that we are opposed to anything that is ethically irresponsible. I at any rate do not think that as a theologian I have any points to make against either the doctor or the lawyer. If Walter Jens and I wanted to do anything, it would be to speak for those doctors, one of whom said to me last week: 'Can you expect me also to say publicly what I have said to you privately about my attitude to active help in dying? If I did I would immediately be prosecuted; there would be headlines in the newspaper, indeed I might even be convicted . . .'

What we need first of all is for those who are not doctors or lawyers, people who cannot simply be said to represent some professional interest, to raise the existential problems and bring about a change in awareness. Here Jens and I are solely interested in helping people today who are terminally ill, and thus of course also medicine and jurisprudence, to remove certain tabus which still exist in the question of active help in dying. I am not for the removal of all tabus, truly. I am fighting for an ethic, and there are ethical questions which must be discussed openly.

Here, Herr Niethammer, I can first most easily indicate our consensus over medicine by means of your four questions.

1. We are fully agreed about the anxiety that so many people have about the dominance of medical apparatus. You have confirmed in a laudably clear way how well-founded this anxiety is in the face of often inhuman treatment. At any rate there is no dispute between us over how much practice in our hospitals leaves to be desired.

Of course I would also agree with your second point. Indeed one cannot foist all the blame for the present situation in our clinics on medicine: it is the concern of the whole of society. We all share the blame for the way in which people are dying in our clinics, often in an inhuman way. Anyone who does not visit a terminally ill person when that is quite possible shares in the guilt. There is no question at all that this is the duty of everyone. And it is too simple to foist the responsibility on to medicine.

Your question 3 was whether active help in dying is the only expedient. There too I would immediately agree with you. Of course not. Jens and I did not give our lectures under the simple slogan 'Active Help in Dying and Nothing Else!' That was not our aim. I had no intention of claiming that this was the only expedient. Of course all your illustrations of concrete help in dying for children meet with my assent. They have simply brought out something which in any case was not an issue among us: that a doctor, in respect of so-called passive help in dying, should do everything in the interest of the patient . . . But in one example you went further: in a particular case you, too, would not have hesitated to give a mortally ill child too high a dose of morphine so that death could result. This is the precise point on which the discussion is focussed: may one do this, indeed should one do it in any circumstances? Can one respond to the request of the patient (or the patient's representative)? That for me is the decisive question to be discussed here.

I differ over your question 4, about the advance directive. I do not think that doctors are the only ones who know death, and that other people get all their knolwedge either from hearsay or from the media. There is surely hardly a family in which one member of the family has not already suffered a slow dying. There will soon be hardly a family in which people do not live to be eighty or even ninety years old. So nowadays there are hardly any young people who have not experienced what the wasting away or the vegetating of an old person is like. Here questions arise which need to be discussed seriously. If the medical side says that in a quite specific case, in some circumstances the doctor can give a dose of morphine which is higher than that is needed to remove the pain, then in effect this would be an instance of the question which moves us. That is the problem which Walter Jens addressed with the example of Sigmund Freud and his doctor.

We can go on to discuss the question of the advance directive later with the lawyer. My view is that such a 'testament' must be respected unconditionally, even by the doctor. And an opinion of the well-known Zurich lawyer Max Keller runs: 'The patient's directive is admissible; it is also binding (on the persons mentioned). The doctor may deviate from it only if he can prove that it does not correspond to what is now in fact the will of the patient; no account should be taken of the possible or hypothetical will of the patient beside his directive. The testator can (validly) commission a third party (as an executor) to see that his directive is observed; the person so charged can execute the directive; the doctor treating the patient may not appeal to medical secrecy in connection with the person mandated.'

I am most grateful to our Freiburg colleague Albin Eser for bringing out in a detailed account what is not disputed by lawyers and at the same time drawing our attention to the fact that there are contradictions over dying and death in the law and in jurisprudence. As he points out, above all, no penalty is incurred if the doctor simply makes available a deadly dose, but as soon as the same doctor personally gives a fatal injection out of compassion the action is criminal and even carries a heavy sentence. These are contradictions.

There is no dispute that there is a whole mass of unresolved questions relating to help in dying. The lines between passive and active help in dying are not clear, and lines which are not clear are unhelpful. Of course I would heavily underline all the reasons that you gave, Herr Eser, in favour of active help in dying; I had already given them in my own contribution. At the same time, in my contribution I also countered some of the reasons given against active help in dying. The argument alleged that this would be a 'breach in the dam' is cited far too often in an attempt to prevent any reform in the law, and the argument of 'misuse' (as in the case of the pill) is too often used to block a better 'use'. The task of the lawyer should be to limit real misuse by concrete regulations and so prevent a real bursting of the dam.

On points of detail, I would want to say. First, I do not think one needs a committee to examine an advance directive. I know from Dutch doctors that even they never make a decision in isolation, but they do not need a committee. They need consultation. A doctor must not do anything here alone; the steadfast will of the dying person must be established, and more than once; the hospital pastor must be involved and also the nurses responsible; only then may the decision be made. So no committee, but a consultation.

Secondly, of course no doctor should be forced to do anything which he or she cannot reconcile with their conscience. My view is the same as yours: no doctor may be forced to offer active help in dying. To this degree I certainly have a right to a dignified dying, but I have no right to a death which could be held against another person (or even against the state). There is a parallel case in law: a woman has a right to abortion in certain circumstances, but this does not represent a right for a particular doctor (or even the state) to carry out the abortion. No, in both cases my right does not entail any obligation on another. Even an advance directive is no basis for a claim to be killed by a quite specific other. However, whether such a doctor must not then in some circumstances say, 'I cannot do it, but I know another doctor who perhaps could help', is a different matter.

Nor need we argue, Herr Eser, over the question of the inviolability of life or, better, the relativity of the safeguarding of life. You know as well as I do what is beyond dispute here, both in law and in moral theology. Even traditional Catholic moral theology has always made it clear that the inviolability of life is in no way unlimited. Three exceptions have always been mentioned. Life is not inviolable 1. in cases of individual self-defence; 2. in the case of the collective defence of a people, i.e. in a defensive war; 3. or in the case of the death penalty, though this has now been abolished in most countries. That means, and here we are presumably agreed, that the inviolability of life is not an absolute right but a relative right, which must be clarified in the individual case.

Similarly, I myself have emphasized that abuses are possible in the case of active help in dying. This is a question for 1. legislation and 2. jurisprudence, so that abuses are prevented as far as possible from the start. In this respect I am in favour of the most restrictive laws possible. But precisely in that situation, first of all the basic ethical problem of principles must be resolved. If someone is in such a bleak position that he or she persistently confirms, 'Really, I cannot go on living, I want to die' – and there are such cases, more than is often conceded –, in the view of a Christian (and I say that quite honestly first of all for myself) do not such people have the right for their desire for help in dying to be respected? Here in principle I want to maintain that as a Christian I affirm responsibility for my life as given by God, and this responsibility applies from the beginning of life to its end. No one today can dispute that here there is an oppressive question for countless people. How does one meet with a good end? The presupposition is that the suffering is really no longer tolerable. If that is the case, then I think that as the person concerned I have the right to determine the time and the manner of my own dying. And then I would be glad if some doctor or someone with medical skills were to help me in an appropriate way.

Walter Jens: I think that we should first of all note that a discussion of the kind that we are having this evening, on a frontier path, leading through tabu zones, would have been impossible even ten years ago. We have made progress, thank God, over the questions: 'What human autonomy is there in the face of death? Is an end put to it a certain point, and who decides this point, who controls it, who has to decide it? Do outsiders have the right to supervise the dying and dictate to them a "thus far and no further" because the moribund person is regarded as an object which is no longer allowed any personal capacity for decision?'

May supposedly well-meaning people, ignoring the wishes of the victim, say to opponents like those cited by Ulrich Bräker in his diary for March 1797, 'Oho, that would be to anticipate the Lord of life and death. That's what the scribes and Pharisees would say to me. It must be left to God; God has laid down an end for everyone and that may not be changed'?

What I ask myself is this, very personally, looking towards my own end. Must one, in the words of Cesare Pavese, let death get one rather than be able to die?

Question upon question arises (as Franz Kafka said, 'Under your rising feet the stairway grows upwards'). After a life which I have determined myself, may I not also have a death I have determined myself, instead of dying as a ridiculous object, only a pale souvenir of myself? Moreover, this last picture will remain, and for those who are left behind will long outlast the impressions of the days when I was an 'I' and not an 'it', a thinking being and not a packet of muscles, not a string puppet, a being whose pride perhaps consisted in his weakness – but a weakness that was thought about and conceded.

However – and this is the decisive question for all of us – how is this small, self-determined 'transition' from here to there to be accomplished? Can one really say definitively at what point passive help in dying – which is allowed – ends and active involvement in the process of dying – which is a criminal offence – begins? How slippery the transition is! How difficult, almost impossible, it is to define the point at which at the passive moves over into the active. 'I'm switching off the apparatus': isn't that already a dramatic intervention? 'I'm putting the fatal dose on the bedside table in the ward': is this planned action really far removed from a readiness *not* to put a medicine that prolongs life on the table? Or, 'I'm giving the patient an injection which contains an increased dose of morphine which will help him quietly to go to sleep': active help in dying? 'I'm putting out a medicine which the patient herself may take.' Passive? Active? 'I'm helping the dying person, at his own request, with a drink.' Active, passive?

However one may decide in a zone the limits of which should be drawn only by considerations of humanity (but who can define its foundations, premises and perspectives?) – one thing is certain. On Herr Niethammer's thesis everything depends on the co-operation of two human beings at the death bed. One asks, one gives; one needs help, one helps – I in the awareness that for the helper, too, the hour will come in which he (or she) needs the help of a third person and this person will need a fourth who will need a fifth: the human chain needs to be preserved over time, a millionfold.

However, in such reflections we should not trivialize the fact that by my insistence on the autonomy of the individual W.J. my wife, my sons, a friend, a pastor (who in the end could just as well give the injection as a doctor) or a colleague from the medical faculty could be caused pangs of conscience. What becomes – and here I am attempting to take Herr Niethammer's thought further – of the autonomy of the partner at the death-bed if he or she has to do what is asked for again and again, and in such a way is determined by outside factors?

In this situation a person (of either sex) comes into play who in the age of increasingly specialized medicine has wrongly faded into the background: the family doctor. Family doctors know their patients, know their dignity and their weaknesses, their suffering and their hypochondrias. And after long, long conversations they can judge what patients can do and what they can no longer be expected to do. They alone, on the basis of past discussions in the last and the penultimate hours, are in a position to judge whether help needs to be given in dying, at home, and not in the clinic.

The ideal family doctor is the one who helps with minor ailments and also with the last and most serious one. There, thanks to a precise knowledge of the patient, his or her background and situation, the family doctor will be able to say, 'I'll help you' . . . perhaps also referring to Ulrich Bräker, who wrote in his diary in March 1797: 'Don't believe that it is against human love or the supreme truth, or that the highest spirits are displeased at such actions.'

The ideal family doctor – that is a person who knows when he or she must tell me the truth and when silence must be kept, for not saying anything also has a dignity. We should praise the doctor who dealt gently with his patient Theodor Storm, after X-rays had inexorably given the diagnosis of cancer, because he knew that his patient could not live with 'We've come to the end.' And so the doctor, supported by the family, revised his statement.

'We were wrong. You can go on living.' Theodor Storm returned to his desk and, although his illness largely limited serious activity, completed his masterpiece *Der Schimmelreiter*. Only then was his work done; the doses of morphine were increased (' I can't go on living', the dying man wrote), though in dying the support which the doctors had given him alive failed him. Storm was left alone, on 4 July 1888, after 5 in the evening. There was no Max Schur to help him.

And we all need a Max Schur, a partner, perhaps already from our youth upwards, in order, as I said in my lecture, to be able to live courageously, because then we shall know that in our dying we shall not have to endure a torment towards which we have to go for decades in fear and anxiety of every kind, minor despondencies or great depressions. Once again, I am arguing emphatically for the problem no longer to be made a criminal offence, not only for the sake of a dignified dying but also and in particular for a dignified living, made possible by a relaxed prospect of the last days.

There may be advantages in having a grey area, under the medical slogan, 'But we've already been doing what you want, my friend, for a long time; however, please don't talk about it, otherwise you'll only damage yourself and me and my colleagues who are doing as I do, but dare not say publicly what we do about help to die in a humane and liberal way.' But I do not want to live with this; my vote is for a precise legal regulation. If one is lacking – and that is what will happen, despite many small and highly welcome steps on the way to a comprehensive solution of the problem – then I fear that a kind of Russian roulette will be played behind the patient's back. If I live in Tübingen, fine; if I live (pardon the choice) in Memmingen, woe is me, because there I shall only find doctors who, unconcerned about their own dying, in which they will cry out to colleagues, think like Dietrich Niethammer, in the style of Bräker's Pharisees, 'Oho, that would be to anticipate the Lord of life and death!'

Therefore, following Herr Eser, my vote is for a decriminalization of help in dying which deserves the name 'dignified', help in a euthanasia on which humanity has to decide here and now – and not the recollection of a praxis which turns good and evil into their opposites.

Dietrich Niethammer: Herr Jens, I think that it has become very clear from what you have just impressively described and also said in your lecture that death is an individual event. We all die our own deaths, as we live our own lives, and all the examples that you have cited are so individual and different that I cannot imagine any legal ruling that would do justice to all of them. The doctor who treated Theodor Storm was his friend. He understood that Storm could only go on living if he repressed the fact of his life-threatening disease, and he would have been a bad doctor if he had gone up to him and said, 'Dear friend, you're suppressing nothing. You must die now and please realize the fact.' Freud once said – just to enlarge on this – that no one can keep on thinking about his death. And how far individuals can accept their death and at what point certainly depends on their own experience.

Herr Küng, I am not quite so certain that there are really so many people in our society who have experienced death at close quarters. Indeed we all know death well enough from television and from newspapers. And of course each of us has relatives and acquaintances who have died. But I don't really know how many have really sat by the bedside of a dying person and thus really experienced what dying means. And that is the decisive thing. When you say that there are hardly any young people who have not experienced what the wasting away or vegetating of an old person can be like, that is one aspect. But supporting someone to the point of death is another side of the coin, and probably the decisive one. And let me make one more point before Herr Eser joins the discussion. We shouldn't succumb to the temptation of trying to bring everything under one heading. I think that there is a clear difference between us, and one which I can respect.

But I must say once again that a legal ruling which gives the patient the right to ask for death or to be killed puts doctors under incredible high moral pressure, whether they take such action or not. For if they are responsible for a patient then – I ask myself – what must they really do if they do not want to kill ten times? If a doctor wants to discover the right thing for a patient and the patient has the right to ask to be killed, then things become difficult. Perhaps this is a point into which Herr Eser could go more deeply.

Albin Eser: Yes, what should a lawyer say, coming after such eloquent speakers as Herr Küng and Herr Jens, or after someone who can report from experience as impressively as Herr Niethammer has done? But perhaps I can still contribute something to legitimate one aspect or another of what has just been discussed.

Herr Niethammer, in agreement with Herr Jens you rightly said that death is an 'individual' event – and Herr Küng had already made a similar point. That is certainly correct as long as one is bringing death on oneself. But as soon as another person is involved, death, too, becomes an interaction between two human beings. So you yourself ended by asking how doctors should behave if the question, indeed even the wish or desire is expressed to them, 'Give me what I need to die or if need be to kill myself.' Here dying and help in dying also becomes a social problem. And whenever there are different answers – as in this question – we have to look for an authority to offer help in deciding; for where unclarity prevails, at least an attempt must be made to achieve more clarity.

Herr Jens has indicated very impressively the difficulty in drawing lines. However, that is so to speak the bread and butter of us lawyers; for as soon as distinctions are made, lines have to be drawn. This 'pain over frontiers' is so acute in the question with which we are concerned because in any distinction one somewhere arrives at a point where it is no longer quite clear that up to this point one should do something that is to be prohibited from this point on. But this 'grey zone of the still or no longer' is nothing unusual; we come up against it literally day and night, if we try to distinguish these two phases. We all know that there is day and there is night. But can you please tell me where day ends and night begins? With good reason, because it is hard to make a verbal distinction here, recourse is constantly had to a particular time to distinguish between day and night. But even this is somewhat arbitrary, since bright moments can possibly already be counted as night, whereas dark moments are still regarded as day. What I want to express with this analogy is simply that if we do not want to leave dying and help in dying simply as a random matter, then we cannot avoid making some distinctions. But if we then draw a line between A and B, there will always be cases in which it can be said that something is contradictory, or not obvious. However, despite these vaguenesses we cannot avoid drawing lines.

I would like to take up one further point to which Herr Jens and Herr Küng in particular referred very impressively, namely that of autonomy. From a legal perspective I do not have particular difficulties in allowing participation in suicide. Certainly I have moral objections to it, but from a legal perspective it can be said that if someone kills himself or herself this is to be respected as an autonomous decision. My difficulties begin with killing on request, because here the responsibility is placed in the hand of a another person: if one takes tablets and thus deliberately kills oneself, then one has made the decision. However, if one leaves the killing to the doctor, then the doctor ultimately takes control of when one dies or does not die. Whether this should really be legalized seems to me to be very problematical, not least on moral grounds. And the advance directive provides only limited help here. Herr Küng has spoken with great vigour about the unconditional need to respect the advance directive. However, the question is, what is really meant by 'respect'? To begin with I had the impression that this meant not only that the doctor *might* observe it, but also that he or she *had to* implement a request to be killed. But later you said that you did not want to force the doctor to yield to the request. In order to remove such lack of clarity, in my view a sharp distinction needs to be made here between 'may' and 'must'. On the one hand if the doctor might stop treatment because the patient wanted this. I would say that this 'may' happen, since to continue treatment of the patient against the patient's will would even be a violation of his or her physical integrity. But it would be different if the respect had to be understood as a 'must', with the consequence that if there was an advance directive to the effect 'I want an end put to my life', the doctor had to meet this request. Here I would see the precise problems that Herr Niethammer has already addressed in arguing that this could be too much for some doctors – in both moral and human terms. So I could only be prepared to accept a regulation which imposed no penalty if a doctor wanted to accede to the patient's request to die; I would be against a regulation that accorded the patient a kind of 'claim' which the doctor then had to meet.

This already brings us to the last point I want to touch on: the question of the right form of regulation. Even in the 'alternative draft' we of course spent a long time considering whether this sphere should not simply be left to the courts, all the more so since the courts themselves are evidently fairly happy with the scope left to them. Therefore it was also extremely illuminating for us to note that the majority of lawyers at the 1986 German lawyers conference thought that we did not need a legal regulation because – like doctors in practice – we can deal with matters in an 'underhand' way, if need be with the help of the courts. However, as a citizen I do not like such a situation much. I would like not only to see the possibility of dying in peace and dignity accorded to the person who has the good fortune to have a doctor friend who knows the best thing to do, but also for it to be possible for this to be done quite openly, rather than benefitting only those who have 'good connections' in this respect. For me, this, too is a matter of equality, since it is about not only equality in life but also equality in leaving life, which can be guaranteed only when there are fairly clear rules. That is also where my criticism of the Dutch ruling begins: it does not tell doctors clearly what they may do in individual cases. This is all the more problematical since the Dutch evidently want to allow not only help in suicide and letting people die, but also in active killing on request. However, if it is nowhere said precisely in what circumstances this may happen, but cases are always to go to the state attorney if death is hastened without the request of the patient, which is evidently the intent in Holland, then doctors are again forced underground, since as a precaution they will not reveal what they are really doing. Therefore much as Holland may be a pioneer for particular developments in some other things, in this respect it has opened a door without having found a way which could satisfy me completely.

Hans Küng: We can now clarify various viewpoints. First let me respond to you, Herr Niethammer. Our question is not whether many people have experienced dying as you or another doctor have experienced it. Otherwise we would have to leave all decisions about life and death to doctors. And that is precisely what we do not want. Even doctors cannot dispute that they do not have the right to decide on whether others should live or die.

In principle we must say – and here I am again quoting the Dutch theologian, Professor Harry Kuitert, who seems to me to have written the best considered book that I have found on the question of active help in dying. Kuitert has formulated the following central principle: 'The right to live and the right to die is the nucleus of self-determination; it is an inalienable right and includes the freedom to decide personally on when and how our end shall come, instead of leaving this decision to others or to the outcome of medical intervention.'

In other words, the adult can, may and should decide personally here. What that means in the specific case will certainly be thought about very carefully. I would largely identify with the well-known alternative draft of a law on help in dying produced by German professors of criminal law and medicine.[1] However, in the first place lawyers should speak on legal questions of precise regulation . . .

Albin Eser: The lawyers may be the guardians, but the will must come from the people.

Hans Küng: You yourself, Herr Eser, have played a part in formulating a statement which I would like to quote here from the alternative draft: 'The court can remit the punishment if the killing serves to end a serious state of suffering which the person concerned can no longer bear which cannot be removed or relieved by other measures.' That is the proposed paragraph 216 section 2. And that is precisely what I also want to say. Here I am also in agreement with the lawyer when he opposes the doctor, who would like to leave all this in a grey area. Why?

First of all, I do not want, quite personally, simply to be delivered over to any kind of medical whim. I do not want to be delivered over to a fate like that of the person a doctor recently told me about when I asked him about a similar case: 'No problem, then you will no longer feel anything, we can make things quite painless. You won't feel a thing.' This is precisely what I do not want. I do not want to lie there possibly for months, even years, without pain and consciousness. And if you should tell me that this is a new view, I can tell you that, as people know, I studied for seven years in Rome under the strict Pius XII. I still remember how in 1952 he gave an address at the International Congress for the Histology and Pathology of the Nervous System. In it, even this conservative Pope condemned the fact that medical measures so prolong life that at the same time the free self-determination of individuals is extinguished. The Pope spoke out clearly against degrading people – and here I quote him literally – 'so that they become no more than conditioned senses or living automata'. That is also my view: and that is what I do not want to experience.

Secondly, I also do not want to experience what another doctor said in a very friendly way to reassure me: 'In some circumstances you no longer feel anything, for example if you have advanced Alzheimer's disease. People can be really happy with it. We have the case of a professor who no longer knows who he is; every day he leaves the clinic and cheerfully goes into the town; he has a number on his back, his telephone number; then he goes to a bar and comes back merry a couple of hours later.' To be honest, I don't want to see myself wandering through Tübingen one day to the amusement of the survivors![2]

So I am for rulings. And I am for rulings not least for the sake of the doctors. I have noted that doctors must be anxious – and their anxiety is well founded – about speaking the truth publicly about active help in dying. What doctors have told me and have told Walter Jens, what we all know, is that they must reckon with being informed on, getting into the newspapers, being entangled in a trial.

I did not say anything when Professor Hackethal published his history of help in dying, because I did not want the publicity. But on the other hand, even then my view was that we cannot allow things to go on like this – without any legal regulation, particularly since on the medical side things are always happening that one assumes would not happen. In other words, we can hear from any number of doctors that in hopeless situations they gave an overdose of morphine when they thought that right. Why can't that be said openly? But if a doctors did say openly what they had done in particular cases, they could be prosecuted and would have to be convicted.

Here is another case: I know of doctors who have made an agreement among themselves as colleagues to help one another actively in dying if it comes to the point. That's among doctors; for us theologians it's not so simple. We can only give one another the *viaticum* . . .

A third case which similarly occurs (it has been made clear to me time and again that the medical profession is split over the case of active help in dying, at any rate today, and things were hardly different ten years ago): only last week a doctor said to me, 'Of course, if it came to it, I would give myself an injection of morphine' (in Tübingen we know of such a case involving a doctor). But why is that possible only for doctors?

The most recent description of the Aids situation which I have been given from America, a report on the most recent investigations from New York, San Francisco and Los Angeles, says the following: 'Among people with Aids it is an open secret. When the time comes, many say that they will make sure that they get control over their own death.' How? Because the members of the 'Aids community' help one another, and everyone knows that one can be helped and that those suffering from Aids will help one another if there is no other way.

These are all instances which one could continue at will and which make me agree with the lawyer. Why should all this be swept under the carpet? Why should the truth for doctors be different publicly from what one can hear in private? Why can't one make the necessary rules and the necessary restrictions legally? Of course I am against any misuse, and I am not one of those – perhaps. Herr Eser, you remember an earlier discussion about 'heterogeneous' artificial fertilization and experiments with embryos – who regard anything that can be done technologically as meaningful and permissible; I find much in this area absolutely abhorrent. In such cases I am in favour of criminal law intervening in some circumstances. So – as I have clearly said – I am against people who have traded in cyanide. But this sort of thing happens when other solutions are not allowed. So I am decidedly in favour of legal regulations, and we should discuss what belongs in such laws and what does not. I know that there are difficult questions to be solved here. But I think that we shall have made a beginning if we talk about them openly, as openly as we are doing in this discussion.

Albin Eser: Herr Niethammer, at this point may I ask a question about medical ethics? If I see things rightly, you also accept the German ruling that help in suicide should go unpunished. But why – and this is my question to you as a doctor – is help in suicide really said to be out of keeping with being a doctor? Couldn't a very large number of wishes to die be met in a humane way by adopting this course? Moreover, it would make it easier for the patient to ask the doctor (who need not necessarily be a personal friend) about this question. But as long as doctors regard help in suicide – and thus even in procuring tablets – as unprofessional, patients who do not want to damage their relations with their doctor will find it a problem whether or not to confront these doctors with such a question. Hence my question: if the medical profession declares help in suicide to be unprofessional, do we then possibly have only a kind of pseudo-holiness, because doctors cannot incur the slightest suspicion of doing something immoral? Or is there a real moral conviction behind the refusal to become involved in suicide? At any rate I could imagine that particularly if involvement in suicides was legitimate for doctors, they could be very much better helpers than the third parties whom the persons concerned are compelled to seek out. Legally the whole thing has been made worse by the fact that according to the law a will to commit suicide must in principle be left out of account, with the consequence that in some circumstances the patient is driven even further into solitude; for if patients are told that their desire to die is to be left out of account, then they may possiblu have the last support that they need taken away from them, because anyone who did not prevent the onset of death would possibly be open to prosecution. In order to counter this fatal consequence for patients, would it not be a step in a better direction for doctors to rethink matters in the direction of more humanity instead of the traditional professional feelings?

Dietrich Niethammer: Herr Eser, I think that in giving help in suicide one is really not very far from giving active help in dying, if it is necessary. But let us think of a person, young or older, who has an acute depression and in this depression wants to die. Should we doctors help such a person? Or should we not? I think, Herr Eser, that we are in full agreement about the aim. What you are saying or what I understand you to say is that the attitude of doctors which you describe leads patients not to take them into account. On the contrary, it forces them into solitude, because it makes clear to them that in certain areas they will get no help from doctors. I think that a bad thing. My plea was and is that we doctors must rethink the fact that we must be responsible for the phase of dying and also a phase of wanting to die. But I would be very much against offering help in suicide as a general possibility which poses no problems. Here too, I think that what happens is again very individual. There are certainly patients in whose cases something like a last or a higher injection of morphine is the only helpful way. I believe that the decisive thing is for patients to learn that in this emergency they can come with their problems to someone who can help them. How that happens you have also, thank God, described in an admirable way: laws should not be made on the basis of the individual instances, since these laws do not make this help in need better, but often probably worse in its final effect.

Walter Jens: Ladies and gentlemen, colleagues, that concludes an enterprise which was not without risk, but which in the end, despite different emphases here and there, has brought us near to a consensus. Two viewpoints are decisive.

First, the problem of a dignified dying must no longer be burdened with tabus. So an end to the term 'addictive', which is so easily hurled into the debate! Away with the rigid apron strings of practical physicians, who are still told by bureaucrats that while the prescription of morphine in large doses could relieve pain, it could also make patients dependent on their drugs! 'Dying addicts' – that is sheer cynicism, and an expression of inhumanity. (Have such people who – but, thank God, they decide less and less – argue like this never thought that they themselves could be in such a position? Doesn't the thought of one's own dying lead to sympathy, i.e. the capacity to feel the death of other persons, suddenly stripped of their otherness?)

And then there is a second point: the decriminalization of help in a dignified dying – beginning with legal immunity for those friends and doctors who make the transition easy for a dying person by offering a cup of hemlock, with reference to one of the most moving deaths in history, that of Socrates.

But what – and here as you rightly point out, Herr Niethammer, the problem begins for the doctor – happens when the dying person can no longer swallow? Then, I think, the doctor who understands his Hippocratic oath the way Max Schur did must go a step further; and here the one fatal injection is decisive, but no less the presence, the physical and psychological presence at that moment.

No, help cannot be laid down normatively nor in a binding way, nor can it be fixed in a way that is generally valid. Every individual case looks different – doctors attending death-beds will be aware just how much, but the fact is also demonstrated by literature, which points beyond the hospitals into everyday life. Literature makes it possible to experience how wretchedly people die, on the gallows, by the equipment of torturers, in the flames of war, in tormenting plagues, 'in bonds' (once again an expression of Ulrich Bräker), in straitjackets in cells for the mentally ill. (Today the tranquillizer silences: 'the main thing,' one keeps hearing hear and there, 'is for the patient to be tranquil'.)

But literature also brings out the other side: help in the hour of death as it is given by the servant Gerassim in Tolstoy's 'Death of Ivan Ilyich', who puts his master to bed, comforts him and looks after him.

As we have seen, only in our century has literature begun to describe dying with the accuracy of autopsies: how people think who stand on the threshold, how they approach, coming from afar and suddenly robbed of all familiar contexts, the hour of being alone, the point from which, in a split second, talk changes from the present to the imperfect: 'Now he is very peaceful', said at 23.04; 'he was composed to the end; he found help; a friend supported him', said at 23.05.

And time and again the question arises which Peter Noll raised in his 'Dictates on Dying and Death': 'Why may animals be put to sleep but not people?' Why – yes, why?! – does not the remark of the Nobel Prizewinner for Physics, Percy Bridgeman, recorded in Sherwin B.Nuland's great essay on dying, find a millionfold echo? 'When the ultimate end is as inevitable as it now appears to be, the individual has a right to ask his doctor to end it for him.' And if not the doctor, then perhaps his own son, a man like Philip Roth, who bent over his dying father to whom he did not want a ventilator to be attached, and whispered, 'Dad, I'm going to have to let you go.'

No, there is no lack of literature to clarify, in a supposedly enlightened time, a problem which has remained in the dark all too long: 'Human dignity is inviolable.' May this statement be expunged when it comes to dying?

Everyday practice, and also the reflection of literature, shows that this cannot be accepted. We must act with dignity: this formula should hold in life but also in connection with a dignified dying.

Postscript. The Encyclical *Evangelium vitae* and the Problem of Help in Dying

Hans Küng

Even very critical contemporaries will agree with some of the statements made by the present Pope in his encyclical *Evangelium vitae*. The Pope is right to point out:

— There must be more respect for life, respect for life as it comes into existence and for handicapped, suffering and dying life.

— Unlimited individualism and autonomism threaten to turn into egotism. This threatens the foundations of human society in matters great and small.

— Freedom can be abused by a mentality of 'Whatever gives pleasure is permissible'. In the long run this must prove destructive, not only for human relationships and society, but also for the ongoing happiness of individuals themselves.

The need for moral commitments

In its 'Declaration on a Global Ethic', the Parliament of the World's Religions which met in Chicago in 1993 started from the presupposition that in the present situation humankind urgently needed a basic ethical orientation: a fundamental consensus on binding values, irrevocable standards and personal attitudes. There was need for an ethical minimum (not ethical minimalism!), which in the first place included a 'commitment to a culture of respect for life' (III.1): 'All people have a right to life, safety, and the free development of personality in so far as they do not injure the rights of others. No one has the right physically or psychically to torture, injure, much less kill, any other human being.'

But if one compares the encyclical *Evangelium vitae* with the 'Declaration on a Global Ethic', it is immediately striking that whereas the latter strives towards a basic ethical consensus between the different religions, indeed even between believers and non-believers, in the former, in an apocalyptic picture painted in black and white, humankind is divided into a 'culture of life' and a 'culture of death' (an expression apparently used for the first time in the church by John O'Connor, a former military chaplain and now Cardinal of New York). All those who have a different view from that of the Pope on questions of contraception, abortion and help in dying belong to this culture of death. For this 'gospel' of the 'representative' focusses on these three points, which do not occur in the gospel of Jesus Christ at all. The Chicago 'Declaration on a Global Ethic' did not take a stand on these three particular points. Why not? Because here there is no consensus, either between the religions or even in any one of the great religions, far less in the Catholic Church.

Of course no one can prohibit a religious leader from taking a stand on these controversial questions as well. Indeed it would even be extraordinarily helpful if a religious leader were to indicate a convincing middle way here, between a libertinistic individualism on the one hand and a traditionalist rigorism on the other. But this Pope, deeply stamped by Augustinian pessimism and dualism, has resolutely chosen the rigorist way. He would have done better to have gone by the remarks of John XXIII, who at the opening of the Second Vatican Council distanced himself from those who 'burn with religious zeal yet do not sufficiently allow a correct assessment or a wise judgment to prevail': 'But we have a quite different view from these prophets of doom who always predict disaster, as though the world were about to come to an end.'

The trap of the ideology of infallibility

However, John Paul II, who grew up under two totalitarian systems, has no inner understanding of Reformation and Enlightenment, and is full of a profound mistrust of the modern world and democracy. 'Prophet of doom' as he is, with a terrible oversimplification, in his encyclical he divides humankind into those who belong to the 'culture of death' and those who belong to the 'culture of life'. Indeed in the tones of a zealot he denounces and criminalizes as 'conspirators against life' all those

- who in a sense of responsible parenthood practise birth control;
- who in questions of pre-natal diagnosis, termination of pregnancy and help in dying with the utmost pangs of conscience decide differently from the Pope;
- who as doctors, nursing staff and advisers help those concerned;
- who as members of parliaments out of inner conviction vote in legislation over abortion, for example, for allowing termination of pregnancy in the first three months.

The irony here is that all this is being said by the former Archbishop of Krakow who, as we now know, was a member of the Papal Commission on Birth Control, though without once having taken part in a session of this important post-conciliar commission. Instead of this, behind the backs of the commission he provided the wavering Paul VI with papers which served as useful preliminary studies for the disastrous encyclical *Humanae vitae*. But the same Pope, who as Pope is inspired by a Polish messianism (the Slavonic Pope), thinks that in the most intimate questions of human life, with an appeal to divine authority, he can deny people freedom of conscience, and indeed deny even democratically elected parliaments the right to pass legislation in this area. He wants from the start 'definitively, and with strict compulsion' (as Bishop Karl Lehmann put it) to seal the lips of bishops and pastors, theologians and those among people and clergy who think otherwise. In particular he wants to silence the theologians. Here we have the voice of a spiritual dictator rather than that of a 'good shepherd'.

Instead of a magisterial orientation we have a magisterial prohibition. The claim is being made that in today's world only the Catholic Church, and in the Catholic Church only the Pope, knows what the truth is. As the *National Catholic Reporter*, the leading organ of American Catholics, remarked critically in a leading article on the encyclical: 'The Catholic Church alone, with the Pope as its sole inerrant voice, possesses and proclaims God's revealed truth. The message now includes the medium. Since there is little new in moral teaching in this encyclical, the newness here (beginning with *Veritatis splendor)* is the Pope's insistence on being the singular vehicle for proclaiming truth. The effect is to raise the stakes and to put papal authority and church credibility on the line' (14 April 1995).

For many Catholics today, this whole claim is grotesque, given all the catastrophically wrong judgments made by Rome in matters of faith and morals, from the cases of Luther and Galileo through the condemnation of Chinese and Indian forms of worship and names for God and the condemnation of historical-critical exegesis and the theory of evolution to the condemnation of freedom of conscience and religion and human rights generally. Yet once again this Roman magisterium proves to be unerringly unteachable. And even Catholics of a traditional disposition are slowly noting the fatal trap in which the First Vatican Council's definition of infallibility in 1870, forced through by Pius IX (the majority of German and French bishops had left Rome previously in protest), has landed us; the church's magisterium cannot be reformed and therefore cannot be corrected.

However, the degree to which this Vatican doctrine has lost credibility even in the Vatican is shown by the astonishing fact that while the present Pope may speak 'infallibly' and mobilize all the authority available to him – the authority of Peter, holy scripture, tradition and an (alleged!) consensus of the church for his most solemn statement on abortion and euthanasia – he does not dare to use the words 'infallible' or *'ex cathedra'* because these have become counter-productive. Here would have been an occasion, finally after the 1950 dogma of Mary, to 'define, declare and decree' dogmatically once again what the 'truth' is.

But what good would this have done a Pope whose support among, say, German Catholics (and the position is similar in other industrialized countries) sank from 79% in 1980 to 16% in 1990 (to the dismay of the German Conference of Bishops). What is the percentage today? If we were to attribute this development, as the Vatican usually does, to the 'Nordic mists' and the Reformation, we would be taught better on this point too by the most recent survey in Catholic France, the land of 'clarity'. In 1994 83% of the French felt that they should go solely by their consciences and just 1% claim still to be guided by the official teaching of the Catholic Church. All in all this indicates the bankruptcy of an ideology of infallibility which in the 125 years since its definition has not only been of no help to the Catholic Church but has immeasurably harmed it. Even bishops all over the world are asking themselves whether the Catholic Church is infallibly on the way to becoming a mega-sect.

The decisive point on euthanasia missed

Now to the specific question of euthanasia. In this encyclical the Pope also gives what in the end is traditional Catholic teaching: 'Certainly the life of the body in its earthly state is not an absolute good for the believer, especially as he may be asked to give up his life for a greater good' (no.47). At the same time he concedes that there can be situations of conflict, like that of an individual or collective emergency, in which attacking the life of another person can be justified. The only remarkable thing is that the same Pope who in addition still allows the imposition of the death penalty for 'cases of absolute necessity, when it would not be possible otherwise to defend society' (no.56) thinks that in questions of help in dying he must advance a thoroughly rigorous view with reference to the sanctity of life (which now once again is made absolute).

Here the encyclical does not introduce any new perspectives into the debate. For the traditional Catholic doctrine is that a person must not use any *media extraordinaria* (inappropriate means) for preserving his or her life, and we knew that already. So the Pope has nothing against not taking measures to maintain life (for example by the use of a ventilator) or stopping such measures in hopeless cases. But the decisive question to be put to this position which allows 'passive help' in dying is: why should the switching off of a ventilator with fatal consequences (= 'passive help in dying') be judged to be morally quite different from increasing a dose of morphine with fatal consequences (= active help in dying)? That is incomprehensible. Doctors, lawyers and theologians are increasingly coming to see this distinction as theoretically contradictory (can an action be passive?) and of little use in practice.

In this book, which appeared in Germany almost at the same time as the encyclical, Walter Jens and I have energetically argued against all human arbitrariness in the question of dying and especially against any outside pressure over dying either from the state (the Nazi euthanasia) or society ('social pressure'). But we have differed from the encyclical, which at the decisive points radiates dogmatic coldness and pitiless rigorism instead of sympathy and solidarity with those concerned, and we have felt it necessary to take new perspectives seriously in assessing the problems connected with dying.

1. As a result of the tremendous success of modern medicine and eugenics, people today have been given what is in fact a new period of life, often lasting more than twenty years. In certain cases, however, this can lead to an undignified decline into vegetation, frequently over many years. In such cases of intolerable suffering it should be possible to help people to ensure that their deaths are not dragged out endlessly and that they can die a dignified death – if that is what they want. There should be no compulsion to die, but there should be no compulsion to live either. We think it arrogant that anyone – a doctor or whoever – should want to decide whether or not a patient feels a situation to be subjectively intolerable. In the end this is something that only the sufferer knows.

2. The problems of this last phase of life cannot be brushed aside with pseudo-arguments: that in reality this wish to die just does not exist; that it is merely foisted on people, and where it is expressed is merely a call for more human support, help and security. Of course everything should be done to give suffering and dying men and women a maximum of human support. That is why Walter Jens and I are also fully behind the efforts of the hospice movement. But even in this movement there are experts who know that (*a*) old people who are suffering express the wish

to die in a well-considered way and by no means simply as the result of a momentary depression, and (*b*) this wish cannot just be seen as something is foisted on them but must be respected as authentic. Shattering testimonies have come to us since the publication of this book in Germany of old people complaining that no one will help them to die and that some doctors just want to talk them out of this desire. What answer is one to give, for example, to an eighty-year-old woman who for almost twenty years has been suffering from an acute case of osteoporosis and constantly has such terrible pains that the desire for a speedy death has been her 'constant companion' for all that time?

3. Palliative medicine has made most welcome progress: it is not only absolutely necessary, but in most cases also extremely helpful. However, it is not the answer to all the questions of life and death. All doctors know this: no therapy to relieve pain is possible without sedation. And the higher the dose (and it must often constantly be increased) and the more it relieves pain, the more sedative its effect is. That means that normally the vigilance, the wakefulness, the spiritual presence of the patient is all the weaker. So our question is: is a person obliged to live away the last 'artificial' phase of his or her life, perfectly 'tranquillized', in some circumstances for weeks, months or even years, dosing away in a twilight state? To reject this certainly does not mean to approve of an unbounded autonomism ('one can make what one will of one's life); it is a plea for conscience and responsibility.

That brings me to the decisive point, which is completely missed in the encyclical. Who has the responsibility for dying? As a believer I know that the life of God is a gift, but I also know that at the same time it is a human responsibility (first of my parents and then my own). One cannot simply 'leave everything to God' at the end of one's life, any more than one can at the beginning. And just as the Roman teaching on birth control has led into a cul-de-sac, so too has its teaching on help in dying. No, human responsibility does not cease in dying, but here is called for one last time, to the degree that a person consciously experiences this phase. And why should I give up responsibility in particular for the last phase, having been asked to be responsible throughout a long life? Why should I not be able to give my life back into God's hands after a mature examination of my conscience? Precisely because a human being never ceases to be a 'person' (here I differ from P. Singer), he or she should be able to make a decision in personal dignity. 'You shall not kill!' Certainly. But here it is not a question of 'murder', which presupposes lower motives and maliciousness. No, what is at issue is the 'surrender' of my own life in full responsibility, and in some circumstances I may be dependent on the help of others to do so.

One last thing: as a theologian I have attempted to develop a new view of dignified dying which I hope will one day be understood even in Rome. Precisely because as a Christian I rely in reasonable trust (= faith) that everything is not over with death, but that I shall be taken up into a last dimension beyond space and time, into the eternal life of God, then in the spirit of the Sermon on the Mount I need not be so terribly 'anxious' about 'adding a cubit' to my span of life (cf. Matt.6.27).

Granted, none of us yet knows what our death will be like and how much courage we shall have to die; every death is different. But we may express a hope that, if ours is not to be a sudden death, we may be able to take leave of this world supported by true friends and with the help of an understanding doctor, in composure and confidence, in gratitude and tranquil expectation.

Notes

A Dignified Dying
Hans Küng

1. M.Heidegger, *Being and Time* (1927), London 1962 reissued Oxford 1967, 289.

2. G. Schulze, *Die Erlebnisgesellschaft. Kultursoziologie der Gegenwart*, Frankfurt 1993, 532.

3. Ibid., 538f.

4. Ibid., 542f.

5. Ibid., 543.

6. Cf. N. Postman, *Amusing Ourselves to Death. Public Discourse in the Age of Show Business*, New York 1985.

7. Cf. E. Kübler-Ross, *On Death and Dying*, London and New York 1969.

8. Cf. R. A. Moody, *Life after Life*, Covington, Ga. 1975.

9. Cf. K. Thomas, *Warum Angst vor dem Sterben?, Erfahrung und Antworten eines Arztes und Seelsorgers*, Freiburg 1980.

10. Cf. E. Wiesenhütter, *Blick nach drüben. Selbsterfahrungen im Sterben*, Gütersloh 1974, 65f.

11. I. Kant, *Critique of Pure Reason* (1781), B 670, ed. N. Kemp Smith, London 1964, p.532.

12. Ibid., B 668f., p.531.

13. Id., *Critique of Practical Reason*, A 265, ed. T. K. Abbott, London 1879, p.357.

14. Id., 'Reflexionen zur Metaphysik', no.4996, in *Kants handschriftlicher Nachlass*, Vol.V, Berlin 1928, 55.

15. F. Nietzsche, 'The Intoxicated Song', *Thus Spoke Zarathustra*, translated R. J. Hollingdale, Harmondsworth 1961, 332.

16. Schulze, *Die Erlebnisgesellschaft* (n.2), 65 (which also contains references to studies of experience by R. A. Easterlin and W. Zapf).

17. Augustine, *Confessions* I.1.1.

18. E. Bloch, *Ergänzungsband zur Gesamtausgabe. Tendenz – Latenz – Utopie*, Frankfurt 1978, 319.

19. Cf. S. Freud, 'The Future of an Illusion', in *Civilization, Society and Religion*, The Penguin Freud Library 12, Harmondsworth 1985, 235.

20. Cf. especially Udana VIII, 3.

21. L. Schmithausen, 'Nirvana', in *Historisches Wörterbuch der Philosophie*, Darmstadt 1984, 854–7: 855.

22. Cf. A. de Condorcet, *Esquisse d'un tableau historique des progrès de l'ésprit humain*, Paris 1794.

23. Cf. K. Oesterle, 'Zum 200. Todestag des letzten Philosophen der Aufklärung', *Schwäbisches Tagblatt*, 14 May 1994.

24. The ten basic principles of a hospice (J. C. Student, following Cohen 1979 and Buckingham 1983):

1. The patient and his or her relations will all be regarded by the staff as under their care.

2. Care by an interdisciplinary team (especially a nurse, doctor, social worker, minister).

3. Round the clock care at hand or at the end of a telephone ('twenty-four hours a day, seven days a week').

4. Thorough knowledge of and experience in the control of symptoms (especially pain relief), taking into account the physical, psychological, social and spiritual dimension of the symptoms.

5. Voluntary helpers as an integral part of the staff.

6. Acceptance of the patient into the programme independently of questions of cost.

7. Continuing care of the bereaved.

8. The staff to be directed medically by the doctor.

9. Co-operation with existing services (clinics, home care, etc.).

10. Permanent cover for the home care staff.

25. The killing of 'empty human shells' and 'ballast existences' for whom human society could not be expected to care had been called for long before Hitler's euthanasia programme by K. Binding and A. Hoche, *Die Freigabe der Vernichtung lebensunwerten Lebens*, Leipzig 1920.

26. Cf. A. Ziegler, 'Sterbehilfe – Grundfragen und Thesen', *Orientierung* 4, 1975, 39–41; 5, 1975, 55–8.

27. The most recent guidelines of the German Federal Medical Bureau for Doctors on care of the dying state (*Deutsches Ärtzeblatt*, 17 September 1993): 'In the case of patients with irreversible illnesses or injuries with an unfavourable prognosis, especially in the terminal stage, the relief of suffering can be so much to the fore that any shortening of life which may possibly result from this may be accepted. The same goes for newborn children with severe deformities incompatible with life. – Measures to prolong life may be stopped if delaying the onset of death represents an unacceptable extension of suffering for the dying person and the basic ailment with its irreversible course can no longer be influenced.'

28. Even according to the statement by the Roman Congregation of the Doctrine of Faith on Euthanasia of 5 May 1980, sick persons themselves are mainly responsible for the last phase of their lives (quoted from *Herder Correspondenz* 34, 1980, 451–4): 'In many cases the situation can be so complicated that doubts arise as to how the principles of moral doctrine are to be applied here. The relevant decisions are to be made by the conscience of the sick person or his legal representative and also by the conscience of the doctors; here the commandments of morality and the many aspects of the specific case have to be kept in mind' (453). 'If other medicines are not available, with the assent of the sick person one may use means which the most recent medical progress has provided, even if they have not yet been sufficiently tried by experiment and are not without danger. The sick person who accepts this can in so doing even give an example of generosity for human wellbeing. Similarly, the use of these means may be stopped if the result does not justify the hope that is placed in them. However, in this decision the legitimate wish of the sick person and his family and the verdict of competent doctors must be noted. These are better able than others to make a rational assessment of whether the expected result corresponds to the use of equipment and personnel and whether the therapy applied to the sick person does not bring pains or complaints out of proportion to the advantages that they can bring the patient' (454).

'When death comes closer and can no longer be prevented by any therapy, one may conscientiously decide to dispense with further attempts at a cure which could result only in a weak or painful prolongation of life, but without terminating the normal help that one owes a sick person in such circumstances. In that case there is no reason why the doctor need have doubts as to whether he has refused help to a person in danger' (ibid).

29. In this respect the guidelines limit themselves to quoting the legal and ethical *status quo*: 'A deliberate shortening of life by interventions which are meant to bring on or accelerate death is illegitimate and criminal, even if it is takes place at the patient's request. The collaboration of a doctor in suicide is against his profession' (ibid.).

30. As a caption for his memorial portrait we chose a sentence from the Book of Wisdom 4.13: 'Someone who has come to fulfilment in a short time has fulfilled long times.'

31. A lecture first given to the International Congress of the Society of University Neurosurgeons at the University in Tübingen in 1988 and then to the American Association of Neurological Surgeons in San Francisco in 1992.

32. Cf. the Declaration of the Congregation for the Doctrine of Faith, 5 May 1980, esp. p.452.

33. This aspect of the question has been clearly worked out by the Protestant theologian W. Neidhart, 'Das Selbstbestimmungsrecht des

Schwerkranken aus der Sicht eines Theologen', in *Schriftenreihe der Schweizerischer Gesellschaft für Gesundheitspolitik* 36, Muri, Switzerland 1994.

34. Cf. P. Singer, *Praktischer Ethik*, Stuttgart 1984; H.Kuhse and P. Singer, *Should the Baby Live? The Problem of Handicapped Infants*, Oxford 1985. Think of all the implications of Singer's terrifying remarks: 'I therefore propose that one should attach no greater value to the life of a foetus than to the life of a non-human being at a similar stage of rationality, self-awareness, capacity for reason, sensibility, etc. As no foetus is a person, no foetus has the same claim to life as a person' (*Praktische Ethik*, 162). For the life of a newborn child this means: '. . . the life of a newborn child thus has less value than the life of a pig, a dog or a chimpanzee' (169). Thus what Singer says about people with severe mental disturbances comes as no surprise: 'So it seems that, for example, the killing of a chimpanzee is worse than the killing of a person with a serious mental disturbance, who is not a person' (135). Almost any decision leading to the death of the unborn or newborn can be justified by such criteria and examples, as they have no right to life and there are always conflicting interests. For a critical discussion of Singer's view cf. H. Hegselmann and R. Merkel (eds.), *Zur Debatte über Euthanasie. Beiträge und Stellungnahmen*, Frankfurt 1991; J.-P. Wils (ed.), *Streitfall Euthanasie. Singer und der 'Verlust des Menschlichen'*, Tübingen 1990. After the Holocaust, the distinction between 'fit to live' and 'unfit to live' can no longer be used neutrally in an 'innocent' way. To regard birth as the limit for the right to life and even to regard a newborn child as not a person seems to me to have no foundation in biology, to be ethically unacceptable and legally pernicious. Handicapped newborn babies and people in a coma are to be respected as human persons.

35. Cf. the account by the parents Joseph and Julia Quinlan, *Karen Ann. The Quinlans Tell Their Story*, New York 1977.

36. In 1991 in the Netherlands, according to the official Remmelink report, 2300 patients were given 'euthanasia' by doctors at their express wish; in a further 400 cases the doctors gave help in suicide; in about 1100 cases they ended the life of those who were 'incapable of deciding' (the number of unreported cases may be considerably higher).

37. Cf. H. Küng and K. J. Kuschel (ed.), *A Global Ethic. The Declaration of the Parliament of the World's Religions*, London and New York 1993, 25.

38. Cf. A. Eser, 'Freiheit zum Sterben – kein Recht auf Tötung', *Juristenzeitung* 41, 1986, 786–95.

39. Cf. I Samuel 31.4.

40. Cf. 'Selbsttötung', *Staatslexikon* IV, Freiburg [7]1988, 1154–63 (E. Seidler – H. Kindt – A. Pieper – B. Stoeckle – A. Eser).

41. This aspect has been described particularly clearly by the French theologian J. Pohier, 'Quitter la vie? Ou etre quitté par elle?', *Gérontologie et société* 58, 1991, 63–9.

42. Cf. H. M. Kuitert, *Een gewenste dood*; German, *Der gewünschte Tod: Euthanasie und humanes Sterben*, Gütersloh 1991, 65f. Cf. the criteria of the Royal Dutch Medical Association formulated as early as 1985. According to the information bulletin about 'Exit' dated 16 October 1993 (Grenchen, Solothurn Canton), this organization for help in dying based in German-speaking Switzerland stands for: 1. the right of human self-determination; 2. the right of sick people freely to decide on medical clinical care; 3. help in voluntary death for the most seriously ill or invalid. It seeks to achieve these aims by: 1. establishing the right of every member to passive help in dying in accordance with his or her advance directive; 2. the direction of Exit hospices (with exclusively palliative care); 3. support in voluntary death for seriously ill and handicapped men and women who want to die.

43. Cf. A. Eser, 'Der Arzt im Spannungsfeld von Recht und Ethik. Zur Problematik "ärztlichen Ermessens"', in O. Marquard et al. (eds.), *Ethische Probleme des ärztlichen Alltags*, Paderborn 1988, 78–103.

44. Cf. the ten-page legal opinion by Professor M. Keller of the University of Zurich. He concludes by answering a question put to him by experts, 'Are advance directives drafted in the form which Exit proposes for its members binding on everyone, namely doctors, hospital doctors and nursing staff?': 'The patient's directive is admissible: it is also binding (on the persons mentioned). The doctor may deviate from it only if he can prove that it does not correspond to what is now in fact the will of the patient; no account should be taken of the possible or hypothetical will of the patient beside his directive. The testator can (validly) commission a third party (as an executor) to see that his directive is observed; the person so charged can execute the directive; the doctor treating the patient may not appeal to medical secrecy in connection with the person mandated.' Contrary to the expectations of those who requested it, the opinion of the Swiss Academy of Medical Sciences given by Professor Jean Guinand of Neunberg and Professor Oliver Guillod of Geneva confirmed that advance directives are binding (it can be obtained from Exit in Grenchen). There have recently also been initiatives in this direction in the Federal Republic of Germany. Thus for example by September 1994 the senior citizens' committee of Böblingen/Württemberg had already sent out 10,000 advance directives. A newspaper article indicates that very recently a further 15,000 enquiries have been received.

45. The most recent example of such an 'ethic of life' favoured by Rome, which continues to work with pseudo-arguments completely in line with the 5 May 1980 Declaration of the Congregation of the Doctrine of Faith, is E. Schockenhoff, *Ethik des Lebens. Ein theologischer Grundriss*, Mainz 1993,

328–40: 331. At any rate, this theologian steers clear of the comparison with Nazi practice which is usual in Rome (the *Osservatore Romano* refused to publish a refutation by the Dutch Christian Democrat Minister of Justice, Ernst Hirsch Ballin, of the sweeping Vatican charges against the new euthanasia legislation of the Dutch Parliament).

46. According to the most recent study in the *British Medical Journal*, on the basis of their own information a third of British doctors have at some time given active help in dying. Almost half of them would be prepared to do so if active help in dying were made legal (press release of May 1994). – While this book was going to press, the report of a referendum in the US state of Oregon held on 8 November 1994 reached me; there, by a majority of 52%, medical help in suicide is allowed on certain conditions. Doctors may not give 'lethal injections', but may prescribe drugs at the request of patients. The sick persons must take these themselves. The condition here is that the patient must have asked for the fatal drug at least three times within fifteen days, once in writing – in the presence of two witnesses. Moreover two doctors need to confirm that the sick person has only six months to live and is of sound mind. Patients suffering from depressions are not to have anything prescribed for them.

47. Cf. J. Backbier and J. Mourits, 'Ist der Deich gebrochen? Die neue Euthanasiegesetzgebung in den Niederlanden', in *Herder Korrespondenz*, 1994, 3, 125–9 (Statement by the Dutch Bishops, 128). Already in the 1986 report on 'Euthanasia and Pastoral Care' produced by the synods of the two great Reformed churches of the Netherlands, the decision to have one's life ended is said in certain cases to be a responsible one.

48. The survey was carried out for the three press organs *Le Monde*, *La Vie* and *L'Actualité religieuse dans le monde* by three leading sociologists of religion (G. Michelat, J. Sutter and J. Potel). Cf. the summary account by A. Woodrow of *Le Monde* in *The Tablet*, 21 May 1994.

49. Cf. A. Auer, 'Probleme der Sterbehilfe aus theologischer Sicht', in Grundmann et al., *Krebsbekämpfung* II, New York 1980, 137–45: 141–3.

50. Cf. J. Fletcher, 'The Patient's Right to Die', in A. B. Downing (ed.), *Euthanasia and the Right to Death. The Case for Voluntary Euthanasia*, London 1969, 61–70. H. M. Kuitert, *Der gewünschte Tod* (n.42); P. Sporken, *Menschlich sterben*, Düsseldorf 1972; id., *Umgang mit Sterben-den*, Düsseldorf ²1975. A. Holderegger, 'A Right to a Freely Chosen Death? Some Theological Considerations', *Concilium* 179, 1985, 95, writes: 'Among theologians this fundamental insight has increasingly given rise to the conviction that there is no other way than establishing the possibility of killing or suicide as one given by the creator along with the actual power of running one's own life, so as to conclude that man has to make the moral judgment of the circumstance in which it is to be regarded as justified and in which it is not.'

51. K. Barth, *Church Dogmatics* III.4, Edinburgh 1961, 410.

52. Cf. Kuitert, *Der gewünschte Tod* (n.42), 69: 'The right to life and the right to die is the nucleus of self-determination; it is an inalienable right and includes the freedom even to decide the time and manner of our end, instead of leaving this decision to others or to the outcome of medical intervention.' On the question of suicide cf. id., *Darf ich mir das Leben nehmen?*, Gütersloh 1990. R.Garventa, *Il suicidio nell'età del nichilismo*, Milan 1994, opens up interesting aspects.

53. Cf. Koheleth 3.1f.

54. The prayer of brother Klaus von Flüe can also be understood as a dying prayer:

'My Lord and my God, take from me all that keeps me from you.

My Lord and my God, give me all that helps me towards you.

My Lord and my God, take me from myself and give me wholly to you.'

For the basic theological questions addressed in this plea see the detailed account in my book *Eternal Life?*, London and New York 1984, reissued 1991.

The Dignity and Indignity of Dying as illuminated by Literature
Walter Jens

1. Cf. the impressive analysis of the events of the passion in J. Blinzler, *Der Prozess Jesu*, Regensburg [4]1969, especially 321ff.

2. Ibid., 327.

3. Ibid., 357ff. Cf. also W. Jens, 'Jesu sieben letzte Worte am Kreuz', in *Zeichen des Kreuzes*, Stuttgart 1994, 11f.

4. E. Jüngel, *Tod*, Stuttgart [3]1973, 133.

5. *Iliad* 22, 369ff., quoted from the version by Richmond Lattimore, Chicago 1951.

6. Ibid., 390ff.

7. Cf. W. Barner, 'Der Tod als Bruder des Schlafs', in R. Winau and H. P. Rosemeier (eds.), *Tod und Sterben*, 144–66.

8. *Der Ackermann aus Böhmen, ein Streit – und Trostgespräch vom Tode*, modern version by Felix Genzmer, Stuttgart 1963, 46.

9. Euripides, *Alcestis*, 172ff.

10. L. Tolstoy, 'The Death of Ivan Ilyich', in *The Death of Ivan Ilyich and Other Stories*, Harmondsworth 1960, 104f.

11. Ibid., 105f.

12. Ibid., 127.

13. C. McCullers, *Clock without Hands*, Harmondsworth 1961, 8f.

14. P. Roth, *Patrimony. A True Story*, London 1991, 16.

15. Tolstoy, 'The Death of Ivan Ilyich' (n.10), 161.

16. McCullers, *Clock without Hands* (n.13), 7.

17. P. Noll, *Diktate über Sterben und Tod. Mit einer Totenrede von Max Frisch*, Munich 1987, 65.

18. Ibid., 63.

19. M. Wander, *Leben wär' ne prima Alternative. Tagebuchaufzeich-nungen und Briefe*, Darmstadt 1980, 198.

20. S. B.Nuland, *How We Die*, New York 1993 and London 1994, 8.

21. Ibid., 10.

22. Ibid., xvii.

23. Ibid., 217.

24. Ibid., 142. For the problem of 'the model for a dignified dying' see also the description of the gentle end of Hubert Humphreys, in E. Shneidman, *In grenzenloser Unempfindlichkeit. Briefe und Zeugnisse von Menschen, die ihren Tod erwarten*, Munich 1987, 195ff.

25. Nuland, *How We Die* (n.20), 241.

26. Ibid., 254. For the problem of help in dying addressed here, above all in the Netherlands, cf. L. Kennedy, *Sterbenshilfe. Ein Plädoyer*, with a preface by Walter Jens, Munich 1991.

27. Nuland, *How We Die* (n.10), 153.

28. McCullers, *Clock without Hands* (n.13), 208.

29. Roth, *Patrimony. A True Story* (n.14), 233.

30. A. Camus, *The Plague*, Harmondsworth 1960, 178. For the problem of death in Camus' work cf. K. Schaub, *Albert Camus und der Tod*, Basel dissertation, Zurich 1968.

31. K. Marti, *Leichenreden*, Neuwied 1969, 23. Cf. C. Mauch, *Poesie – Theologie – Politik. Studien zu Kurt Marti*, Tübingen 1992, 96–120.

32. U. P. Haemmerli, 'Medizin und Menschenrechte', in W. Höfer (ed.), *Leben müssen – sterben dürfen. Die letzten Dinge, die letzten Stunden*, Bergisch Gladbach 1977, 155–77.

33. U. Bräker, *Tagebücher und Wanderberichte. Der grosse Lavater Gespräche im Reich der Toten. Etwas über William Shakespeare's Schauspiele*, ed. S. Voellmy and H. Weder, Zurich 1978, 38f.

34. M. Schur, *Sigmund Freud, Leben und Sterben*, Frankfurt am Main 1973, 620. For the same topic see also *Letzte Tage: Sterbegeschichten aus zwei Jahrtausenden*, ed. H. J. Schulz, Munich1988, 46–55 (Joachim Cremerius on Sigmund Freud).

35. Cf. S. Freud, 'Thoughts for the Times on War and Death', in *Civilization, Society and Religion*, The Penguin Freud Library 12, Harmondsworth 1985, 85 ('Our unconscious does not believe in its own death: it behaves as if it were immortal'). Cf. Tolstoy, 'The Death of Ivan

Ilyich' (n.10), 137: 'In the depths of his heart he knew that he was dying but, so far from growing used to the idea, he simply did not and could not grasp it. The example of a syllogism which he had learned in Kiezewetter's *Logic*: "Caius is a man, men are mortal, therefore Caius is mortal," had seemed to him all his life to be true as applied to Caius but certainly not as regards himself. That Caius – man in the abstract – was mortal, was perfectly correct; but he was not Caius, nor man in the abstract: he had always been a creature quite, quite different from all others . . . Caius was certainly mortal, and it was right for him to die; but for me, little Vanya, Ivan Ilyich, with all my thoughts and emotions – it's a different matter altogether. It cannot be that I ought to die. That would be too terrible.'

36. Cf. H. Schipperges, 'Das Phänomen Tod', in *Der Tod in der Dichtung, Philosophie und Kunst*, ed. H. H. Jansen, Darmstadt 1978, 12–20 (on Petrus Hispanus and his *ars vivendi*, 15).

37. K. Marti, 'Wie gemsen wie fische', in *Schon wieder, einmal; Ausgewählte Gedichte 1959–1980*, Darmstadt 1982, 67.

Dignified Dying from a Doctor's Perspective
Dietrich Niethammer

1. Cf. P. Noll, *Diktate über Sterben und Tod. Mit einer Totenrede von Max Frisch*, Munich 1987.

2. Cf. R. Leuenberger, *Der Tod. Schicksal und Aufgabe*, Zurich 1973.

3. Cf. S. B. Nuland, *How We Die*, New York and London 1993.

4. Cf. E. Kübler-Ross, *Reif werden zum Tode*, Stuttgart 1976.

5. Cf. P. Roth, *Patrimony. A True Story*, London 1991.

6. P. Sporken, quoted by F. Böckle (n.7).

7. F. Böckle, 'Menschenwürdig sterben', in *Ärtzliches Urteilen und Handeln. Zur Grundlegung einer medizinischen Ethik*, ed. L. Hanefelder and G. Rager, Frankfurt 1994.

The Possibilities and Limits of Help in Dying:
A Lawyer's View
Albin Eser

This contribution is based on the following works, which give full details of sources: A. Eser, *Suizid und Euthanasie als human- und sozialwissenschaftliches Problem*, Stuttgart 1976, 392–407; A. Auer, H. Menzel and A. Eser, *Zwischen Heilauftrag und Sterbehilfe. Zum Behandlungsabbruch aus ethischer, medizinischer und rechtlicher Sicht*, Cologne 1977, 72–145. For the Wittig case in particular see my 'Sterbewille und ärtzliche Verant-wortung', *Medizinrecht* 1, 1985, 6–17, and for more recent discussion on reform see my 'Freiheit zum Sterben Kein Recht auf Tötung', *Juristenzeitung* 17, 1986, 786–96.

An Open Discussion

1. *Alternativentwurf eines Gesetzes über Sterbehilfe*, proposed by J. Baumann, H. Bochnik, A.-E. Brauneck, R.-P. Callies, G. Carstensen, A. Eser, H.-P. Jensen, A. Kaufmann, U. Klug, H.-G. Koch, M. von Lutterotti, M. Perels, K. Rolinski, C. Roxin, H. Schöch, W. Schöne, H. Schüler-Springorum, H.-L. Schreiber, J. Theyssen, J. Wawerski, G. Wolfslast, K.-J. Zülch, Stuttgart 1986.

2. Critical questions were asked about this remark after the discussion. Nothing was further from my mind than to say that the amazing care of patients with Alzheimer's disease was superfluous. I wanted primarily to speak solely for myself, but in so doing to argue in principle for the right of self-determination in this case as well, as long as the patient was still capable of making a decision. That Alzheimer's disease is anything but harmless and that it can be a complete psychological and physical shock to those suffering from it and be a heavy burden on relatives for years is impressively described by S. B. Nuland, *How We Die*, New York 1993 and London 1994, Chapter V, 'Alzheimer's Disease'. Here is a significant question which again raises acutely the question with which I am concerned. Must a patient allow all this to happen, or does he or she have the right, before such a situation develops, to put an end to his or her doomed life, in full awareness, with the help of a doctor? Nuland writes:

'As more time passes, patients will gradually slide toward complete dependency. Those who do not succumb to such an intercurrent process as stroke or myocardial infarction will very likely lapse into a condition that has been termed, inhumanly and yet very descriptively, the vegetative state. At that point, all higher brain functions have been lost. Even before then, some patients are unable to chew, walk, or even swallow their own secretions. Attempts to feed may result in spells of coughing and choking which are frightening to watch, especially when the observer feels at fault. This is the period when hard decisions are faced by families, having to do with the insertions of feeding tubes and the vigour with which medical measures should be taken to fend off those natural process that descend like jackals – or perhaps like friends – on debilitated people.

If it is decided not to tube-feed, death by starvation may be a merciful choice for people who are unconscious or otherwise without sensation of the process. Starvation may well seem preferable to the alternatives, the paralysis and malnutrition that almost inevitably overtake even the most scrupulously fed of intubated terminally ill people. Incontinence, immobility and low levels of blood protein make it almost impossible to avoid bed sores, which can become ghastly to look at as they deepen to the point of exposing muscle, tendon, and even bone, coated in layers of foul, dying tissue and pus. When that happens, the psychological trauma on the family is mitigated only a little by the knowledge that its victim is unaware of it.

Incontinence, immobility and the need to catheterize lead to urinary-tract infections. The inability to acknowledge or to swallow secretions causes aspiration of mucus and increases the likelihood of pneumonia. Here again, difficult treatment decisions must be made, involving not only individual conscience but religious beliefs, societal norms, and medical ethics. Sometimes, the best course may be not to make those decisions and to let grim nature have its way' (104).

Acknowledgments

Permission is gratefully acknowledged for quotations from the following books:

Sherwin B. Nuland, *How We Die*, Alfred A. Knopf, New York 1993

Philip Roth, *Patrimony*, Jonathan Cape 1991